John Olson
April 2012
Bainbridge Island

Down John's Road

Down John's Road

Recreating John Steinbeck's 1960
American Road Trip

John R. Olson

DEDICATION

To my wife and best friend Lisa – a trusted partner in life, without whom nothing of merit I ever accomplished was possible.

CONTENTS

PROLOGUE

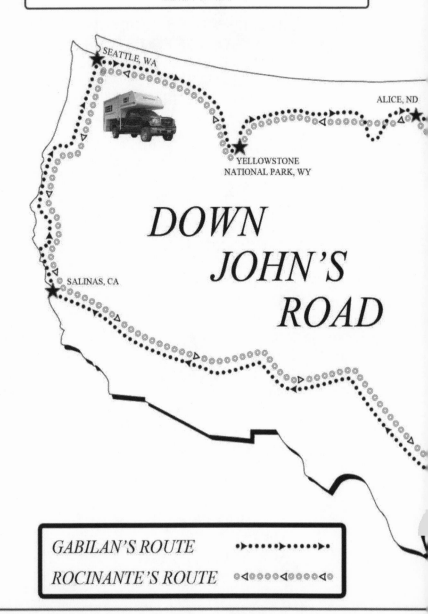

TWO MEN. TWO TRUCKS. TWO AMERICAS.
1960-2009

SEATTLE, WA

ALICE, ND

YELLOWSTONE
NATIONAL PARK, WY

DOWN
JOHN'S
ROAD

SALINAS, CA

GABILAN'S ROUTE

ROCINANTE'S ROUTE

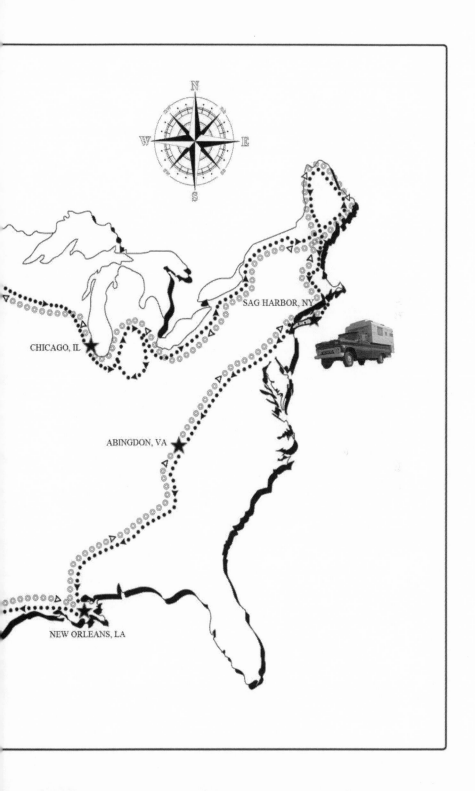

PROLOGUE

Not all those who wander, are lost.

J.R.R. Tolkien

****

John Steinbeck rescued me.

In October 2008, a financial calamity, fed by live-beyond-your-means Americans, greedy investment banks, and inattentive regulators strangled my dreams. Retired as a journalist, I had planned to buy an RV, hug the centerline and see America. But when my modest portfolio tanked by one-third and gas zoomed to $4.40 a gallon, the open road was visible only in Sunday newspaper travel sections.

Then, the rescue. From his iconic *Travels with Charley* – replete with a dignified French Standard poodle, new GMC pickup truck, and innate ability to get lost surrounded by maps, John Steinbeck wrapped my dreams anew. It took a ribbon 12,000 miles long.

On September 23, 1960, Steinbeck began an eleven-week journey through thirty-four states. Almost five decades later, I decided to reprise his journey – as close in method and means as Steinbeck himself.

I would beg, borrow, or steal a GMC pickup truck; put a camper on back and head out, disdaining with equal scorn Interstates, chain hotels and fast food. At shotgun, would be Zorro, my trusty Black Labrador, surely as stately a traveling partner as Steinbeck's poodle. Neither of our bladders lasts beyond two hours and Zorro didn't quibble over radio stations as long as two meals a day arrived on time.

John Steinbeck and I were matched in temperament and tenor. He was fifty-eight years old when he left Sag Harbor, New York aboard Rocinante, his truck-camper named after Don Quixote's horse. Steinbeck had been sideswiped by a recent stroke and other health problems. It did nothing to temper his wanderlust, but left relatives and friends questioning his sanity in planning a 10,000-mile trip.

I would be fifty-seven leaving September 2009 from my Puget Sound homeport of Poulsbo, Washington. My health was also a question, having ended a two-year trial of cardiologists, neurologists, and CT scans. It left me saddled with a pacemaker and a mysterious autoimmune malady. Steinbeck and I both had teenage sons who had driven us one step over the cuckoo's nest navigating them to manhood.

Steinbeck no doubt stared into the maw of mortality and felt it best to fight back with Detroit horsepower under his right foot and a loyal dog beside. I too felt the best way to rage against unsolicited AARP mailings was to take the only road forward I could – the one never traveled before.

Wives couldn't keep us home when eclectic gas stations, greasy-spoon cafes and true tales of Joe Average American beckoned.

John Steinbeck and I went careening down America's back roads and highways, five decades apart, connected by a cup of joe, newspapers, and infinite curiosity.

What Steinbeck found around the next bend of the road in 1960 is the sinew of his jaunty, best-selling book *Travels with Charley.* I was no Steinbeck when I drifted out my driveway on a foggy September 1, 2009. My bona fides were that I had visited forty-five states by car, covering 40,000 miles. I knew how to journey, but I was a retired newspaper editor, not an author.

A Rand McNally atlas would be my North Star. The only woman along was the insistent voice cooing from my Garmin GPS. My heart would capture with my eyes what my digital camera could not with its lens.

County crews had paved the road out of my neighborhood just days before departure. The asphalt felt like ice cream absorbing my oversized Michelin tires and five-ton rig as I glided over the stretch of road I had traveled for two decades.

The first miles from home were all too familiar. The slick roadway was the closest thing to a departing red carpet I would get.

With that self-delusion, I was gone – *down John's road.*

1 ROAD TRIPS WITHOUT END

If you don't know where you are going,
then everything is a surprise – an elation.

Thomas Steinbeck

****

It was just an audiobook. Yet my life changed the day narrator Ron McLarty uttered the last words of John Steinbeck's *Travels with Charley:*

And that's how the traveler came home again.

Traveling began for me in the mid-1960s when a new Chevrolet Impala cost $3,500 tops and Elvis was still in the building. My family took a trip in Wisconsin from which, essentially, I never returned. My mailman father announced we would cram into our two-door, 1954 Chevrolet Bel Air and go camping. To me, the journey was Marco Polo leaving Venice for China. In reality, it was two hours long.

From that trip forward, being home was to wonder when the next journey would begin. The very notion of travel, of a new road, became a reason to exist.

So it was in 2009, nearing sixty years old, my urge to drive beyond the next bend was as compelling as the day in the 1960s, when my father's rhythmic three-on-the-tree brown Chevy crunched down our gravel driveway.

****

The travel bug is an affliction to many Americans. It only abates with movement, motion, and the hum of an engine; the spin of crankshafts and tires creating the endless drone of the highway. Stuck in the here and now, the only outlet for a travel muse is more gas, black coffee, and Fed-Ex and Walmart trucks drifting off centerline after midnight. The I-system proves as reliable a travel partner as a Brooks & Dunn CD.

I have taken road trips with purpose and others with none at all. I left Wisconsin in 1972 with two friends in a new Mercury Capri and my first credit card. Our sole purpose was finding a nude beach in Venice, California. We'd read about it, it must be there. We found it, gawked, and then drove back home; an expensive titillation for sure.

After joining the Navy in 1977 and selling the Capri, I blew every penny to my name on a two-week trip to Canada and the East Coast. Why not? The roads beckoned and my best friend from high school signed up for the journey. I would not need the car or the money in boot camp.

In 1981, traveling between Navy duty stations in San Diego and Germany, I blew through $1,000 and a month of leave with only one purpose; using as many modes of transportation as I could. I drove, rode a ferry, climbed aboard Amtrak, and endured long Greyhound Bus and Pan Am 747 rides, before arriving in Germany – the berserk driving capital of the world with its no-speed-limit Autobahn.

What of those travels? It was sand between my toes ogling naked women at Venice Beach. Sand again as I knelt in the desert outside Cairo mimicking the Sphinx. It was flying over Spandau Prison in Berlin in an Army helicopter watching the sole inmate, Nazi Rudolph Hess, tend his garden. I herded sheep in New Zealand, climbed Mount Fuji in Japan, and kissed my future wife for the first time on the steps of The Louvre in Paris.

It is beyond my comprehension that my great-grandparents never traveled fifty miles beyond their Wisconsin farm, except once, to the 1933 Chicago World's Fair. Was I from the same gene pool?

Any single journey is never enough. The travel urge can't be quenched. It can only be vented, endured. There is always another road, another stretch of highway. Or, another city you can neither spell nor pronounce filled with newness. There is always another rise in the landscape, which, as Robert Frost and Lance Armstrong both might say, makes all the difference.

****

When I retired as a journalist in 2003, I was spent. Too many newspaper press deadlines, too many radio news deadlines as the seconds clicked to airtime. I was going to take a grocery store job lining up cans of tomato soup. Or perhaps work in a bookstore, blowing dust off old classics.

It never happened. Within weeks I was back on the road. My wife was a traveling nurse in Puget Sound and needed a chauffeur to move her between nursing homes, rehab centers and medical facilities. Even a close and familiar road is an open road. I got the job.

When my wife took an inside job at our local hospital emergency room, I hit the road again, this time delivering new and used vehicles in the Pacific Northwest. Auto dealers paid me to drive cars with plastic on the seats, price stickers on the windows, and less than ten miles on the odometer. Still, it only tamped down the urge of the open road.

In early October 2008, the Dow Jones Industrial Average, my own DNA, and John Steinbeck changed everything. Several years before, my wife had checked out *Travels with Charley* as a book on tape. Narrator Ron McLarty read the lilting words about Steinbeck's blacktop circumnavigation of the nation. The book was a commercial success for

Steinbeck, on par with *Grapes of Wrath, East of Eden,* or *Of Mice and Men.*

It was my introduction to Rocinante, the name Steinbeck chose for his GMC truck and camper. Plots were hatched to purchase an RV, any RV. I began visiting mid-winter RV shows in Seattle.

On October 7, 2008, staring at an Internet screen late at night, the stock market was in free-fall. My dwindling portfolio painfully siphoned away my personal Rocinante. I could ill afford even a small RV. My sons' college funds and at least nominal retirement income were more important.

I had been reading a book about the Donner Party traipsing across America to its morbid dead-end in the high Sierras of California. I began thinking of the other great Westward-ho seekers, among them Wells Fargo stagecoach drivers, Pony Express riders, and wagon train masters. Perhaps I could find a way to reprise their journeys, and get magazines and newspapers to buy my articles. There would be no fancy RV, but I would be on the road.

At that very moment, the genesis of the John Steinbeck idea crackled through my synapses. What about *Travels with Charley?* What about Rocinante? Why not Rocinante? After a few Google clicks and peek at the U.S. map, the concept began roiling in my mind. The idea would not only put me in my Rocinante, but in Steinbeck's as well.

The plan was simple in creation, daunting in formation. I would reprise his journey, write a book and publish exactly fifty years after Steinbeck scratched Charley's ears in the front seat of his green GMC.

Steinbeck was fifty-eight when he left Sag Harbor. I would be fifty-eight when my book was published. The idea took hold. I was hell-bent, obsessed, enmeshed in it. Had to buy a GMC truck from Detroit. Had to find a Wolverine camper made in Michigan. Had to study Steinbeck's route. Had to find a book agent, a publisher.

Truth told, what I really had to do was go *down John's road*.

2   THE STATE OF THE ECONOMY

*We want this camper to be perfect. I don't want the
windows to fall out on some highway in Texas and
read about that in Chapter Thirteen of your book.*

Howard Smith Sr., President,
Wolverine Campers.

****

It is easy to *say* you are going to recreate Steinbeck's
Travels with Charley, write a book and live enriched
ever after. In fact, it is not easy.

Unless, of course you *are* John Steinbeck, with the Pulitzer
Prize on your wall, author of multiple best sellers, friend of

presents and publishers alike. When Steinbeck created his journey in his mind, he knew his name alone carried a certain clout in the publishing and business world. Steinbeck said in *Travels with Charley:*

I wrote the head office of a great corporation which manufactures trucks. I specified my purpose and my needs. I wanted a three-quarter-ton pick-up truck, capable of going anywhere under possibly rigorous conditions, and on this truck I wanted a little house built like the cabin of a small boat.

I tried a similar tack, with dissimilar results.

My plan was to write General Motors as Steinbeck did. On October 27, 2008, I sent a letter to GMC Vice-President of Global Communications Steven J. Harris. At the time, GMC CEO Rick Wagoner was beleaguered trying to save GMC from bankruptcy. He couldn't be bothered.

Though I didn't expect to see a 2008 truck arrive in my driveway on the shores of Puget Sound, I had hoped for help from GMC. What I received was what I deserved. An e-mail arrived two weeks later from Debbie Frakes, a GMC-Buick-Pontiac spokesperson:

"Dear Mr. Olson,
Steve Harris forwarded your letter regarding your plan to recreate John Steinbeck's trip across the country in a GMC truck. What a wonderful opportunity for you!

●●▶●●●●●▶●●●●●▶●●●●●▶●●●●●▶●●●●●▶●●●●●▶●●●●●▶●●

I can help you purchase a GMC truck by giving you the same substantial discount we provide our suppliers. If you're interested, all I need is your date of birth and zip code. As you can imagine, given the state of the economy and our company, I unfortunately could not loan or donate a vehicle to you.

I appreciate your understanding. Thanks for your letter and if you're interested in purchasing one of our great GMC trucks, which, by the way, are the most fuel efficient in the industry, please contact me."

After fulfilling Ms. Frakes' requirements, she sent me the coding to present any GMC dealer for a modest discount. Not exactly the treatment Steinbeck received fifty years before. Not exactly a door slam either.

The search for a camper began. From *Travels with Charley*, I gleaned Steinbeck's rig had been built by a firm called Wolverine Campers in Gladwin, Michigan. At the time, GMC had a marketing venture with Wolverine. One could buy a GMC truck with a camper already attached.

Most RV Web sites in 2008 referred to any Wolverine Camper as an orphan; RV jargon for a company out of business. It implies replacement parts are hard to find. Still, I would not give up on Wolverine Campers. Perhaps there was a used one somewhere.

While searching obscure business Web sites for Michigan, I found Wolverine Campers with a phone number. That seemed odd for a company out of business since 1980.

Immediately, I called. Company President Howard Smith Sr. answered.

"Wolverine."

"Is this Wolverine Campers in Gladwin, Michigan?"

"Sure is."

"Are you the company that built John Steinbeck's camper for *Travels with Charley* back in the late 1950s?"

"That's us. I think there is a picture on the wall around here somewhere."

After stifling my joy that the company still existed, I remember telling Mr. Smith one thing.

"Well, get ready to build another one."

"Be glad to."

Just as John Steinbeck had done in the 1960s, "specifications" were discussed by phone, mail, and occasionally by fax. Wolverine Campers did not have a computer on the premises, I would later learn. A price was agreed to, and in January 2009, I took a red-eye flight to Detroit. A precariously icy drive on unfamiliar roads led to Gladwin the next morning. Mr. Smith proved to be an engaging gentleman of sixty-five, and revealed that he had worked at Wolverine Campers as a high-schooler in the late 1950s.

"They didn't trust me to do too much. I think I may have helped rivet the metal on the sides whenever a camper was finished."

On a subsequent trip to Gladwin, Smith showed me the unpretentious white cinder block building on Cedar Avenue where Wolverine was headquartered in the late 1950s. It was there, Smith believes, Steinbeck's Rocinante was built.

From January to June 2009, Smith, his son Howard Jr., and a sub-committee of children, grandchildren and two aging Wolverine employees, Stan and Ernie, hand-built my camper. Inside, it mimicked, as much as possible how John Steinbeck described his own camper five decades before:

... a little house with double bed, a four-burner stove, a heater, refrigerator and lights operating on butane, a chemical toilet, closet space, storage space, windows screened against insects...

My camper would have a shower, a decided advantage over Steinbeck's. He had to stop every few days at a motel/hotel to become presentable for church on Sunday.

The process of ordering my camper and working with the Smith family of Wolverine Campers was a dream, compared to the grinding process of finding the correct GMC three-quarter ton pickup truck.

First, a green pickup like Steinbeck's was out of the question. GMC didn't offer green trucks in 2009. But the myriad combinations of trucks, beds, engines, transmissions, options, tires, wheels, colors, and trim packages was more than my pacemaker-driven heart could endure.

One night in April 2009, the process had begun to weigh heavily, not on my checkbook or finances, but on my heart and blood pressure.

New truck or used? Take advantage of the GMC discount or not? Three-quarter ton or one ton? Regular cab, extended cab, or crew cab? Long bed, regular bed, or short bed? Two-wheel or four-wheel drive? Diesel engine or gasoline? SL, SLE, or SLT trim package? Gray, black, red or blue?

The combo of truck packages GMC offered, when laid on sheets of paper, would stretch from GMC's Detroit headquarters to plants in Pontiac and Flint. The process overwhelmed me.

I called my oldest son, a former car sales manager, looking for advice, if not outright rescue. On a Friday night, I told him how much money I was willing to spend.

"Just find me a truck. I can't do it anymore."

The next day he called.

"Dad, I've just spent three hours on the Internet. I've done some research, made some calls and here's the deal. There's a nice truck in Illinois that might work for you. There's another one in Pennsylvania that might work as well. But the truck you really want is in a little town in Georgia."

I couldn't thank him enough for lifting my burden, even though the black pearl of a nearly new 2008 GMC in Canton, Georgia exceeded my budget by $4,000.

The private owner knocked $900 off his asking price saying, "I decided to sign on for the ride of this book idea of yours."

With that, I flew to Atlanta with a cashier's check next to my anxious heart. The deal was made and I drove through a velvet spring in the south, up over the Mason-Dixon Line to Michigan. I could have stopped at Louisville to watch the

16

Kentucky Derby, but settled for listening on the radio while watching live thoroughbred colts scamper in verdant fields around Lexington, Kentucky.

Dropping the truck off in Gladwin at Wolverine Campers, after a quick inspection of camper progress, I flew home. The plan was to return in a month for pick up. It was not to be. Delays crept into the schedule and my impatience must have been apparent to Howard Smith Sr.

One day, as I asked again about delays, he laconically told me his philosophy.

"John, we want this camper to be perfect. I don't want the windows to fall out on some highway in Texas and read about that in Chapter Thirteen of your book."

His logic was sound, if not eloquent. We came to the conclusion the camper would be done *when it was done*.

Finally Smith called.

"The camper is finished. It went on like a glove. It came off like a glove. It's looking pretty good."

In late May 2009, again I flew to Gladwin via Chicago and Saginaw. Documents were signed, training commenced on the "little house on wheels" and I began my quick journey west to get the rig home.

GMC executive Frakes had written back in November that GMC trucks "are the most fuel efficient in the industry." They may well be, but not with a full-size camper taxing the groaning suspension. My 353-horsepower engine protested mightily against prevailing winds through seven states on U.S. Route 2. Despite a variety of hastily learned hypermiling techniques (coasting down long grades, drafting semi-trucks), I averaged nine point nine mpg. A friend aptly described driving cross county in a camper as "like driving a wall." Arriving home, I had two months for outfitting.

One last assurance had been collected between Michigan and Puget Sound. In my mind, I had to settle a question. Could I uncover the mix of people, events, and sights Steinbeck did in 1960? Did the back roads and waysides still provide an intriguing cross section of the U.S.? Did Obama's America mirror John Kennedy's Camelot? The answer was a resounding yes. Though intent on getting home quickly, I found:

- At midnight, a one-armed man in Bemidji, Minnesota, age forty, playing slow-pitch softball with the vigor and athletic ability of men much younger.
- An oil-company baker from Czechoslovakia driving an aging, belching RV from Alaska to Missouri to relocate a female friend with two cats. His entire gas budget had been decimated and he was stuck in Minot, North Dakota. He had not made it to Missouri yet. Time to fry a few doughnuts.
- Newlyweds from Canada, both RCMP constables. They fawned over each other in lawn chairs in a Walmart parking lot headed to the Grand Canyon, proving Niagara Falls had lost its honeymoon luster.

The country was still out there and still *out there*. During his 1960 journey, Steinbeck wrote that *Teen Angel* whined on his truck radio from Maine to Montana *down John's road.*

On my short trek home, a country music platinum hit by Billy Currington blared through seven states. It reduced life to: *God is great, beer is good and people are crazy.*

Yes.

But only in America!

3 OUTFITTING

*Don't let a woman get involved in the thing. Next
thing you know, you'll need some twelve-function
food processor.*

Thomas Steinbeck,
on outfitting.

****

Trip planning consumed me after October 2008. By
June 2009, truck and camper glistened in my yard,
needing only final outfitting. Travel for me includes

minimal creature comforts. I did not feel pressured to pack. It could wait until the dog days of August, just prior to a September departure.

Maps and atlases became allies as I mentally traveled roads, crossed state lines, and plotted Steinbeck waypoints. Though no map of Steinbeck's 1960 route is known to exist, it can be recreated by painstaking reading of *Travels with Charley*. I had something better.

Steinbeck's route has never been more fully researched than by Herb Behrens, a volunteer at the National Steinbeck Center in Salinas, California. The result is a thick document. He gave me a copy during a visit in March 2009. I cherished it, created a special binder, and though I had yet to drive a single mile of Steinbeck's journey, its pages became dog-eared victims of constant route checking.

At no small effort, Behrens had superimposed pages from Steinbeck's book onto pages from Google Maps. Where Steinbeck mentioned, say, Skowhegan, Maine, Behrens had copied that paragraph from *Travels with Charley* at the bottom of a Google Map for Skowhegan. It proved invaluable. My appreciation to Behrens runs deep.

For weeks, I searched for authentic 1960s road maps. Gasoline companies had printed them by the millions. They could only be had from collectors for a small fortune on the Internet. Thus, Behrens' document, a 2010 Rand McNally Atlas, and my well-used *Travels with Charley* copy became my sextants. Plus, I sheepishly admit, a Garmin Nuvi GPS. Thomas Steinbeck told me his father would have used one in 1960, had it been available:

He would have loved laptops. GPS? Absolutely. But he hated phones. To him, they were a last resort, a necessary evil.

Two pre-departure phone interviews with Thomas proved priceless. Through contacts in Salinas, Thomas agreed to talk from his Santa Barbara, California home. I'm grateful as he was in the middle of intense publication discussions for his second novel *In the Shadow of the Cypress.*

He took time to recall in detail his father's 1960 trip, especially outfitting and pre-trip planning. Thomas said:

Don't let a women get involved in the thing. Next thing you know, you'll need some twelve-function food processor.

John Steinbeck traveled weighted down. I am the opposite, insisting on traveling light. There would be no tossing of junk off my rig 1,000 miles down the road. If it was aboard, it would be used. No *what ifs,* no redundancies. Emergency equipment would be minimal. The truck and camper were brand new, I reasoned, what could go wrong? I had supreme confidence in General Motors and Wolverine Campers.

Steinbeck had no such confidence during final outfitting in late summer 1960. As he left Sag Harbor, his truck camper truly *sag*-ged. He considered himself a tinkerer and packed Rocinante like a mechanic's Noah's Ark - with two of every tool. He had so much gear aboard, Rocinante became a rolling testament to the Craftsman aisle at Sears & Roebuck. His suspension groaned.

He paid a heavy price later with a tire blow-out in Oregon. In standing water, he struggled to change it. He noticed the other rear tire was about to blow as well. Miraculously, on a rainy Sunday in Oregon, a helpful mechanic found two heavy-duty tires. Steinbeck wrote they should have been on there "in the first place."

Steinbeck admitted he had stowed too much. To his defense, today's lattice of convenience stores in our twenty-four seven economy did not exist along his highways. There were plenty of Shell and Standard Oil gas stations where attendants knew something about a vehicle. I took all that into consideration, plus this from Thomas Steinbeck:

If you need something, buy it on the road.

Minimal me cobbled together a small toolbox, even tinier first-aid kit and called it a day. Having gotten less than ten mpg on my trip from Michigan to Washington, I was determined to shed weight. Squeezing fifteen mpg on the big journey was my hope. By late August, everything was aboard, but not one item more.

My GMC Sierra performed perfectly. No warning or caution lights or dreaded *Check Engine* lights came on the entire trip. However, due to my electronic ineptitude, my key fob caused the security alarm to blare a symphony in whatever neighborhood I was in at the time.

Many camper cupboards were empty when I tossed off lines September 1. That would be handy later when I needed space for my daily newspaper addiction; a need-for-news

Steinbeck shared as well. My stack of eighty newspapers eventually filled two overhead bins. They provided valuable background later.

My intention was to cook nightly. But *Food Channel* camera crews would have found scant evidence I cooked at all. Four boxes of Hamburger Helper left with me. Two returned. I used only two pans from a spiffy new set. The oven was operated only a handful of times for mini-pizzas. I had every utensil known to Paula Dean, new pots and pans, microwave, and an RVers cookbook. For the most part they gathered dust. I lost 20 pounds.

With two of my sons, I took a three-day shakedown trip to the Pacific Ocean. That was all I needed.

According to Thomas Steinbeck, his father and third wife Elaine camped once, perhaps twice. Once his father knew how everything worked, there was no need to practice, Thomas said.

Eventually, Elaine sewed curtains and Thomas installed the gun rack:

The gun rack and the khaki clothes and blending in, that was all hooey, a McGuffin. He was out to meet people, get their story. Get information.

Steinbeck originally wanted to drive an English Land Rover Safari Wagon. One was obtained on loan from a dealership, but the Steinbeck family couldn't figure out how to outfit it "without wrecking it." Thomas said it went fifty-five mph tops and that "downhill."

It was wise his father discarded the Land Rover idea, Thomas said, as there were few U.S. dealerships in 1960. GMC dealers abounded. Did his father visit any prior to buying his truck?

That was not my father's style. He would have said 'send me a catalogue.'

Truck campers were coming on the scene in the late 1950s and drew Steinbeck's attention. He might have seen one around Sag Harbor and made inquiries. It's also possible his father read about them in an outdoor magazine, Thomas said:

You couldn't escape a Field & Stream magazine back then if you wanted to get any dental work done.

His father's camper was not custom-built, Thomas said. It just arrived one day in Sag Harbor. That is corroborated by current Wolverine Campers owner Howard Smith Sr. who said no one talked about a celebrity camper coming through the modest Michigan assembly factory in the 1950s. He said Steinbeck's camper may have come from a dealership on Long Island as Wolverine had several outlets in New York.

****

On Bluff Point in Sag Harbor, as Steinbeck prepped for his trip, a young neighborhood boy hung around watching. Eventually the boy begged to come along. The answer was no, but Steinbeck said later he might have enjoyed the lad's company.

In summer 2009, a neighborhood girl and I had become friends. Maggie was eight years old. We shared a love of soccer and sports in general. She followed my outfitting and I told her early on "You can't come along, Maggie. So don't ask." Turns out she had no interest in stowing away, but was intrigued by the process.

One day I asked her to help name the rig.

"*Black Beauty*," she quipped

That was a working name for several days, until a vision of Elizabeth Taylor riding shotgun for 10,000 plus miles nixed that. Without telling Maggie, I rejected the name. I preferred a horse name. Several factors were at play.

First, driving the truck with a heavy camper aboard, a soothing sensation set in. You could feel and hear it above the road din. The camper rode in the truck bed like a new saddle on a swift and powerful horse. When the truck bounced, or veered left or right, there was the sense of a jockey aboard a thoroughbred. It was squishy, in the cowboy way.

Recently, after a forty-year gap, I had reconnected with my old high school basketball coach. "Coach" had also been my senior class English teacher. The only book I remembered him teaching was Steinbeck's *The Red Pony*. In 1970, its nuances were beyond my limited literary aptitude. The name of the pony escaped me, but research revealed Gabilan, a name Steinbeck derived from a mountain range near Salinas.

Gabilan it would be. A black vinyl stencil was created. Maggie and my wife applied the letters to the right rear camper panel; exactly where Rocinante is stenciled on the original camper.

With outfitting finished and naming rights settled, one consideration remained. Would my Black Labrador Retriever Zorro make the jaunt? Though a jocular title for my project had been *Travels with Zorro*, from the outset, prospects were dim for my dog coming along.

Zorro is not the refined travel partner Charley was. Bluntly, Zorro is high maintenance. He yelps or employs a half-dozen other canine yips in a vehicle. He will jump in vehicles readily, but skittishness sets in with a yap piercing your inner ear like a soprano with a megaphone. After consulting books, magazines, dog trainers and trying every method to quiet a canine, his road companionship was abandoned.

I remember the very moment I decided. A mile-long bridge over Puget Sound's Hood Canal had recently reopened. One night, near midnight, I took Zorro on one last training mission to test his nerves and mine. Halfway across the bridge, which floats over a deep natural fjord, Zorro panicked. He jumped into my lap, his furry frame completely blocking my vision.

Quickly pushing him aside, I resolved: "That's it Zorro. You're not going along."

I don't think he understood or cared. He would have made my trip less lonely, but the price would have been steep. Simply put, it would have a cost a great deal of freedom.

27

Twice, Charley grew ill on Steinbeck's trip. Steinbeck expressed anxiety about Charley's health and had to deal with veterinarians in Spokane, Washington and Amarillo, Texas. Charley was also banished to kennels on occasion. Way too much hassle for me.

My eighty-day separation from Zorro was not adverse. I rarely thought of him on the trip, and true to his loyal breed, our friendship picked up exactly where it left off. Labrador Retrievers are like that.

Charley was among the most famous dogs of his era along with Lassie and Rin Tin Tin. But a dog named Marley remains the most famous literary dog of the Twenty-First Century. Zorro nestled under my feet as I wrote this book, little knowing or understanding the role he might have played, if he could have shut his yap.

****

I set up a small business corporation duly registered with the state of Washington. A budget was conceived and funds deposited for gas, lodging, food and sundries.

Departure day loomed September 1, 2009. I wanted to leave September 23, the exact day Steinbeck had departed from Long Island forty-nine years before. A family wedding invitation scuttled that plan.

Those nuptials were planned for September 12 in Waupaca, Wisconsin. I intended hightailing across the northern states for the ceremony and then slowing down for the final eighty days. I had other commitments in the

Midwest as well. Little did I know how much this Midwest amble would muddle my journey's pace and eventually my state of mind.

Then, just before departure, a forewarned phenomenon hit. Steinbeck felt it in August 1960:

In long-range planning for a trip, I think there is a private conviction that it won't happen. As the day approached, my warm bed and comfortable house grew increasingly desirable and my dear wife incalculably precious.

Doubt, like a drippy Seattle winter rain, settled over my soul. Dread crept in and was hard to shake. It involved my wife. A nurse and the family's primary wage earner since I left newspaper journalism five years before, suffered a head injury in 2008 from a fall. For a year she worked at a nearby hospital, while taking post-injury treatments.

By June 2009, it became too much. The therapies, medications and parade of doctors could not remedy the debilitating nausea, dizziness, migraines and sensory overload. She gave up her job. Our income stopped cold. Expenses did not. My wife insisted I take the journey I had so diligently planned.

What had been an opportunity to emulate Steinbeck now became a necessity. This unbalanced the mental equation. Savings and investments dwindled alarmingly. I'd spent $50,000 on a dream, which morphed into something else.

Sleepless nights were the norm. Unlike Steinbeck, with a publisher awaiting every paragraph, I was an unproven author.

How could I leave my wife behind? How could I write a book? How could I reverse our family's financial peril? How, how, how?

One afternoon I begged God to give me a sign. Was the trip misguided, however well-intentioned? Sure, I had Steinbeck's exact truck, camper, and route. I had talked with his sole surviving son twice. Countless hours of research had been completed.

Yet my journey was blurring, contorting, and disconnecting. I could not think of fifty people willing to pay twenty dollars for a travel book written by me. But there sat Gabilan.

On my knees, hunched before my sofa, wracked by emotion, surrounded by the pure weight of it all, I could only ask myself, who in the Bible had set out on a similar journey?

To my mind came Saul, on the road to Damascus in Acts, Chapter 9.

Immediately I read the story of Saul's conversion to Christianity and becoming Paul. After being blinded by a heavenly flash, Paul asked "Who are you, Lord?"

"I am Jesus, whom you are persecuting. Now get up and go into the city, and you will be told what you must do."

It was the answer I sought and the only one God could give. Just go. I would be told. Not until that moment, did I truly believe the trip would happen. I had the means, method, maybe even the moxie.

Leaving my small fishing village west of Seattle, I would go *down John's road.*

4 CIRCLES OF FAMILIARITY

I wonder why progress looks so much like destruction.

John Steinbeck

****

I t was time to depart. From the day the idea entered my mind, it took forty-seven weeks to devise a do-over of *Travels with Charley*. It required a fair bit of traveling itself; three trips to Michigan and one each to California and Georgia.

Fortuitous things happened. I had talked with John Steinbeck's only surviving son Thomas – twice. There was a handshake with a man who possibly, fifty years before, had put rivets or turned screws in Steinbeck's original camper. I had seen Rocinante sitting serenely inside Steinbeck's hometown museum in Salinas, California.

My dog had been fired as a travel companion before riding a single mile. Creating a small legal corporation for taxes, I had spent more money than an unemployed man ought to. Waiting for the trip to begin, I'd pored over maps like Dwight Eisenhower going to war.

Psychologically, I thought I had worked through the perils of solitary life on the road, little knowing the dark edges of loneliness waiting.

Perhaps I went too far getting inside Steinbeck's mind to understand the manner in which he traveled. A pragmatic man, I don't believe in ghosts, reincarnation, channeling, or the extra-sensory world. Yet at times it seemed my thoughts whispered to Steinbeck at night, and his to me.

It was definitely time to go.

At seven a.m. on September 1, 2009, I kissed my pretty wife, petted my dog, and drove east of my comfortable life. It was fifty-three degrees on a day that would soar to ninety-five. I skirted the Norwegian fishing village of Poulsbo, Washington. It would be eight weeks before I arrived in Sag Harbor, Long Island, and the former whaling port Steinbeck departed from.

It began raining for the first time in weeks. Sunshine flickered through clouds as well. The physics of meteorology dictated a rainbow somewhere. If there was, I didn't see it. My camper blocked my rear view. Not that I was looking back.

My route would put me on a ferry within minutes. Not a small, dozen-car boat such as Steinbeck took from Sag Harbor to Shelter Island, Long Island. Waiting dockside for me was the hulking *MV Spokane* capable of carrying 2,000 passengers.

Memory told me the first person Steinbeck referred to in his book was a Navy sailor who said he was shipping out aboard a nuclear submarine from New London, Connecticut.

My hopes were high and chances good of also meeting a submariner. One of the U.S. Navy's largest submarine bases is at Bangor, Washington – five minutes from my home. Salmon, Starbucks and sailors are everywhere in my corner of Puget Sound. After easing Gabilan aboard the ferry at Kingston, Washington, I saw a sailor climb out of a small red Nissan pickup truck. He was in uniform, my luck was running. By the time my rig was properly parked, he had disappeared into the ramble of morning passengers.

No worry. On the ferry's top level, coffee and breakfast awaited any hungry sailor or commuter wanting a better view of approaching Edmonds. I searched fore and aft, but did not find the sailor. I returned to my rig, keeping an eye out for him.

When he returned at the end of the crossing, I sauntered over and found barriers. His laptop computer rested against the steering wheel. He was talking on a cell phone, with an earplug in one ear and his window firmly up.

The slowing *Spokane* approached its slip. What could I do? It seemed intrusive to ask him to roll down the window. My chance at talking to the sailor was blocked in the same manner much personal communication is today. People are so tethered to cell phones, Bluetooth, MP3 players, iPods and laptops, that real conversation with someone two feet away can't be bothered with. I walked away.

Forging through Edmonds to Everett, Washington on I-5, I clocked Interstate miles I wanted earnestly to avoid. Monotonous overhead signs, concrete overpasses, and bland fast food disinterested me.

****

When Steinbeck reached Seattle in 1960, he was at his trip's mid-point. It was my starting point. Steinbeck had been in Seattle twenty years earlier, but now lamented how the city with a "matchless harborage" had changed. There was more traffic. County lanes with roadside berries were now wire fences and factories. Yellow smoke was everywhere. Steinbeck lamented it all:

This Seattle was not something changed that I once knew. It was a new thing. Set down there not knowing it was Seattle, I could not have told where I was. Everywhere frantic growth, a carcinomatous growth. Bulldozers rolled up the green forests and heaped the resulting trash for burning. The torn white lumber from concrete forms was piled beside gray walls. I wonder why progress looks so much like destruction.

●●▶●●●●●●▶●●●●●▶●●●●●●▶●●●●●▶●●●●●▶●●●●●●▶●●●●●▶●●

I too had visited Seattle long before actually moving to Puget Sound. It was May 1978 and I was a young sailor aboard the Navy destroyer *USS Buchanan* making port call. For the three-day visit, I had sixty dollars to spend. I walked Seattle's rainy cobblestone streets, took a ferry to Bremerton to visit the venerable battleship *USS Missouri* and ended up hungry at the Space Needle. Up the futuristic spire I rode and spent one-third my entire budget on a meal in a swank revolving restaurant. Strange miniature ice cream cones were served between courses. I inquired.

"That sir is a depalatizer," said the waiter with white towel over his elbow.

"A de-whatalizer?"

Clearly, I was a sailor out of his culinary league.

Surrounding the base of the Space Needle, a folk festival was ongoing – a festival that continues to this day. The city and I got along well, despite twenty-dollar ice cream cones. I vowed to someday return, which I did permanently a decade later.

If Steinbeck could see downtown Seattle now, to his keen observer's eye it would be even more frenetic. The Columbia Center was the tallest building west of the Mississippi River when completed in 1985. In the last decade, two magnificent sports stadiums costing a combined one billion dollars have been built near its waterfront.

In 1960, Seattle's economy was Boeing and white-collar engineers with plastic pen protectors in shirt pockets. They were building 707s then, and in 2009, the troublesome 787.

Behind schedule and over budget, the extremely high-tech Dreamliner was causing headaches across Puget Sound. On the day I departed, Boeing had just announced a new manager of its commercial airplane division. Boeing tried to put a smiling face on the departure of the past manager, but it didn't work with one industry analyst.

"It doesn't give one confidence," the analyst was quoted in *The Seattle Times*. "If you really thought you were over the hump, you'd wait around for the victory lap."

Ouch.

Boeing is still the top employer, but it has been joined by tens of thousands of Microsoft and Alaska Airlines employees with the casual but important nuance of Starbucks coffee in hand. Seattle baristas crank out frothy blends twenty-four seven.

The U.S. Census listed Seattle's 1960 population at 557,087; in 2009, 609,000. Not exactly meteoric growth, but Seattle's regional clout reigns supreme. Competitors Portland, Boise or Spokane are hundreds of miles distant.

****

Zooming north of the Emerald City, I exited at Everett and said goodbye to I-5. I would not drive it again for 10,000 miles. Veering onto U.S. 2, the towns of Sultan, Gold Bar and Startup flashed by, the latter with a post office no bigger than a living room.

Near Leavenworth, Washington, I stopped for my first coffee refill and found notes my wife and son had slipped me. Reading them, I cried. My wife wrote:

I am so proud of you! You have done your research. You have worked very hard, assembling the countless items needed for this trip. You can set out with confidence. We will be here cheering you on when you pull up into the driveway with bugs in your grille and countless stories to tell.

Then my seventeen-year-old son chirped in:

So have fun, be free and don't worry about a thing. I love you and want you to know that you deserve this trip. You have provided so much and sacrificed for all of us. No one deserves this more than you. So relax and just let your odyssey happen and have the words flow.

No husband or father could have been more touched. I wondered if Elaine or Thomas Steinbeck had slipped encouraging notes into Rocinante in September 1960.

****

Around noon, near Wenatchee, a deer crossed the road. My father often said deer only make appearances at dawn and dusk. This large buck did not get that memo.

As I left the Cascade Mountains, a rich farming tableau awaited. One truck-farm store outside Quincy, Washington had a sign Steinbeck might have seen fifty years ago, with one exception: *Corn, Grapes, Flowers, Apples, Peaches, Wine, Shakes and Espresso.*

Washington is a giant experiment in which God placed every climate imaginable. Not much appears in the other forty-nine states that can't be found in the state of Washington: beaches, mountains, deserts, rain forests, grain fields, apple orchards, rivers, canyons, and occasionally, an erupting volcano.

Nearly forty years ago, I was a student at the University of Wisconsin which had just built a high-tech Biotron to create any climate on earth. In the two decades living here, I came to think of Washington as a living, breathing Biotron.

Outside the small town of Odessa was a tidy cemetery, flat, orderly and verdant. Along the back fence of the cemetery was an aging U.S. Army tank, a tribute to fallen servicemen. One gravesite, which seemed temporary among tiny white stones, indicated three elderly people had all died in June 1993. I stopped at a gas station seeking details of those deaths. The owner and his son were stumped.

"Besides, that's not the story of that cemetery," the older man said. "The Floch boys are buried there. That was the largest funeral this town ever saw. Perhaps that it will ever see. It was something."

The younger man said Odessa was doubly hit in late-summer 2001, when two Floch brothers, their cousin and grandfather all died in a tragic fishing accident off the Washington coast at La Push.

●●▶●●●●●▶●●●●●▶●●●●●▶●●●●●▶●●●●●▶●●●●●▶●●●●●▶●●

"Then 9/11 happened just a couple of weeks later. Man that was a bad time for us. We lost the Floch boys and then the nation lost a lot more. In many ways this town has never recovered."

****

The first day ended for me at a Spokane, Washington Walmart exhausted after 319 meandering miles. When John Steinbeck went to the back of his rig after his first day, a ream of paper had broken loose and sheet-like confetti covered the floor of Rocinante.

As I opened my camper the first night, my new laptop computer had broken loose and splayed out on the floor. The batteries had fallen out and plastic doors were ajar. Had I broken my computer on the first day, ruining its 100,000 reams-of-paper capacity? After reassembling components, luckily it still worked.

Steinbeck said he could not "write hot" - the same day an event happened. He could afford to wait until he returned to Long Island to begin writing.

That was not an option for me. Daily I would need stories, people and events to populate the pages of my future book. I had to write hot. White hot. With the cost of buying Gabilan and my family's finances dwindling, my computer would get fired up nightly.

Near midnight, I lay in bed under the high-glare lights of Walmart – like a false full moon illuminating its parking lot. That day's journey had covered familiar roads through well-recognized towns and cities. Upon departure these roads run out like low-pressure isobars on a weather map, tight and close together. Succeeding days found roads getting longer, larger and more spread out. Everything turns new. Familiar becomes foreign. The circles of familiarity disappear.

****

After a quick passage through Idaho the next day, Montana offered the B-towns: Butte, Bozeman, and Billings. A series of off-beat encounters began. I dubbed them *Midnights at Walmart* and they occurred repeatedly from coast-to-coast.

Just ahead lay a surprise rendezvous with a paroled felon, who earned gas money capturing feral cats and stray dogs with his bare hands. He was one-half of the winsome couple I nicknamed Bonnie and Clyde *down John's road.*

●●▶●●●●●▶●●●●●▶●●●●●▶●●●●●▶●●●●●▶●●●●●▶●●●●●▶●●

5   SONG OF SEPTEMBER

We are playing with the hand we were
dealt. It's what you gotta do.

Tiffany in Billings, Montana,
on being homeless.

****

The three B-towns of western Montana always confuse me. Driving east, which town comes first, last, in the middle? Billings? Butte? Bozeman?

As I drove toward the B-towns, I tried not to conquer the miles which is the male prerogative. To drive, simply *to drive,* is not my style.

A conqueror of miles sees an eighteen-wheeler whistling by. I see much more and questions arise.

What trucking company is written on the side? Werner? J.B. Hunt? Swift? Is it a short-haul trucker or a long-haul? Does a woman sit in the driver's seat? That's rare, so all the more fascinating to see a female wrestle the wheel.

Where is the homeport of the semi-tractor? Oklahoma, Tennessee, or Utah? Usually, it is scripted on the driver's door. Is it a dry goods truck, a reefer, or a flatbed? Does the operator care about appearance? Often semi-trucks fall either side of an extreme; squeaky clean or layered in dirt and dust.

What's inside? Cucumbers or carrots? Lawnmowers or lawn seed? How long has the driver been driving? Where is the rig bound?

My trip would be ninety percent over before I dedicated a day to talking with truck drivers in Winslow, Arizona. Long-haul trucking intrigues me; a story for another chapter.

When a car passes, I often give it a journalist's once-over; an eight-second rolling interview.

Is a family inside? A lone salesman or district manager? Is the license plate local or long distance? Does serenity reign in the car, or are the kids engaged in backseat civil war? Has the family dog lapped his tongue print on the windows? Innocuous questions all, but monotony breakers at sixty mph.

Do other long-distance travelers stay in the moment? See the road, feel the road and think about who's around at any moment? Cars, pickups, trucks, buses, semis, and RVs are individual blood cells in the veins of roads. What other way is there to see them?

One day at noon, I stopped in Superior, Montana. Walking around, I saw the usual downtown establishments: a tavern, church and bank.

Then I spied two plaques on a building that had seen better days. Both boasted Superior was site of the first hotel to receive a Gideons Bible in 1908. Gideons have since distributed Bibles in 180 countries in eighty languages.

The nearest business was a boutique offering herbs, teas, books, candles or haircuts and salon treatments in back rooms. The counter clerk had been in town a year and had never seen, much less read the Gideons plaques.

It wouldn't be the last time I found residents of a town blissfully unaware of significant events or places around them. Many could not point me to an important landmark right under their nose. I call them the "incurious." People, who are born, live and die in a place, yet are ignorant of its significance in place and time.

How could one walk by two plaques every day for a year and never read them? The inquisitive journalist in me rages at the incurious. For the clerk not to know something first happened underfoot, since repeated one point six billion times worldwide, is baffling in the extreme.

****

Departing Butte, the city of red buildings retreated against golden hills as I drove east toward Beaverhead National Forest. Ascending, I turned and looked back into a valley. A Monopoly board emerged. The houses, cabins, trailer homes, small factories and businesses jutted up from a barren landscape like so many houses and hotels earning rent on Baltic Avenue and Park Place.

In *Travels with Charley*, Steinbeck devoted pages to the mobile home phenomenon. Steinbeck did not take a pro or con stance, calling them an unusual and ubiquitous trend.

My own roadside amazement centered on casinos which created a blizzard of the neon emporiums of game and chance.

During a morning stop at a Butte, Montana gas station, my head swiveled at casinos on every corner. In range of a good toss of craps dice stood: Montana Lil's Casino, Montana Club Casino, Magic Diamond Casino and Chances R Casino.

They are often disguised as gas stations, convenience stores, fishing and hunting outlets, restaurants, or even men's clubs. They are what they are – casinos. In Butte, customers had found them by nine a.m.

Thomas Steinbeck said his father was neutral on gambling:

He was never big at gambling. My father was old school and somehow always thought it was best to earn your money. He was not against a rags-to-riches story, but it had to be earned, not bestowed.

Thomas said he has nothing against gambling either, especially tribal casinos:

We took from them. They are just taking from us.

●●►●●●●●►●●●●●►●●●●●►●●●●●►●●●●●►●●●●●►●●●●●►●●

****

After loping along I-90 for hours I was immersed in "Big Sky Country." A turn off the freeway and Yellowstone National Park began pulling me on a gentle upslope for seventy miles toward West Yellowstone. Oncoming traffic whizzed by just feet away as Interstate medians evaporated. Passing RVs and buses made Gabilan lurch.

As I rose 8,000 feet to Yellowstone, fly fishermen appeared. Around any bend, a pickup truck would be parked in a way that allowed quick movement. Then off in the distance, fishermen plied their craft with flicks of the wrist. Lolling in streams with wet suits, water reached their ankles, waists, or for the fully brave, the chest. Cast once, twice, three times. Time after time, mile after mile, the gentle whip and snap of the line, but never did I see a fish rise to the bait.

Did that matter to these fishermen? What were their thoughts as they waded along on the now-cloudless day? Each man in his rubber waders, dressed in brown or green, casting bag at side, worked the stream. Worked the fish. Worked the fly. Always, working, working, working.

****

Steinbeck, in *Travels with Charley*, claimed because National Parks are so unique, with steep waterfalls, deep canyons and soaring cliffs, they are almost the *freaks of our nation*, and no more representative of the United States than Disneyland.

These are harsh words from a man who loved nature. Today what would Steinbeck say is real America? Wrigley Field in Chicago? The Mall of America in the Twin Cities? If Yellowstone is not America, nothing is. Yellowstone preserves an America uncovered by concrete, unfettered by commerce and unpolluted.

Well, almost unpolluted.

Inside Yellowstone, traffic snarled and finally stopped. Perhaps a bear and cubs, an elk herd, or buffalo? Anything could stop a line of cars here. Gawkers and cameras are part and parcel of Yellowstone.

An hour later, I learned a Hazmat team was working a small paint spill. Hazmat was an unknown word to Steinbeck sauntering through Yellowstone in 1960. It would be three years before Rachel Carson's *The Silent Spring* launched environmentalism.

However small the incident, the jarring combination of paint spill, Yellowstone, and Hazmat rattled my sensibilities.

****

Camping in Yellowstone only one night, it was long enough to prove Six Degrees of Separation Theory. The woman camped next to me, with her husband and an entire kennel of dogs in tow, was born in the same small Wisconsin hospital I was six decades ago.

Driving slowly through the park on departure, a herd of buffalo came within four feet of my rig. They didn't care. Neither did the sizable herd of elk I saw chewing their cud at

47

Mammoth Hot Springs on the Post Office lawn. Paparazzi tourists clicked photos, but a groundskeeper took the elk in stride.

"They come down in late summer because the grass is green and tourists friendly," he said.

Rolling out of Yellowstone, I passed through Gardiner, Montana and returned to a rolling American commercial: *Budget Hotel. Budget Rental. Wild West Raft Rides. Outlaw Pizza. AAA Approved RV Park.*

My destination of Livingston, Montana was where John Steinbeck bought a jacket in 1960. I had no need for one, but looked around for Steinbeck's store. A likely candidate? The Mercantile.

Yellowstone had been forty-six degrees at daybreak. Arriving late afternoon in Billings' 100-degree weather, it proved perfect for Friday Night Lights. *The Billings Gazette* promised a high school football game.

A full moon rose over Daylis Stadium as Bozeman High School tangled with Billings West. Bozeman's Hawks posed no match, losing to West's Golden Bears thirty-six to twenty.

The Billings quarterback tossed four touchdowns; his receivers hardly noticed the sponsor's emblem at midfield. But there it was: *Wendy's*.

Americana written in ground beef.

****

While parking at Walmart in Billings around midnight, a couple drove up in a 1984 Ford Econoline van as I leveled my rig with orange, drive-on blocks. Dan and Tiffany questioned my blocks. I questioned them.

"What are the blocks for?" Dan asked.

"They keep the rig level. The fridge, stove, all the water systems love level ground."

"They look cool."

"Thanks. What are you guys doing here this late at night?"

"At midnight, we go in and get our Food Stamps reloaded."

"Reloaded?"

"Yah, they put the money on a card. Like a debit card."

"Where do you guys live?"

"Here," said Dan, pointing to the van. I offered them breakfast if they returned for an eight a.m. interview.

"Sure," they said. By two a.m. they were back. The free breakfast offer worked its charm.

We talked the next morning in my camper over Egg McMuffins. They ate. Fast. Furiously fast. Egg bits and biscuit crumbs flew. They hadn't read Emily Post's *Etiquette* lately. I didn't mind, I wanted their story.

"Did you guys graduate from high school here?"

"I dropped out," Dan said. "I was into a lot of crime. Whatever I could do to make money. My dad didn't care. He did at first, but he just gave up. I did a felony and did prison time for two years and got out about two years ago. I'm just trying to get my life going straight. I was a day away from rookie training for firefighting and I crushed my foot in a rollover. I tried flagging, but I would sit on my lunch pail and get in trouble. I have had surgery. I have partial nerve damage. Part of my foot is still numb. When I walk, I wobble. And when I stand on my foot too long, it starts aching. All my bones were piled up. It was a puzzle they had to put back together."

I asked how he paid for the surgery.

"Well I'm bi-polar. I get mental health insurance to pay for all my medications. I owe $90,000 for my foot. I guess I'll pay it back a dollar at a time."

Dan did his time at a Deer Lodge, Montana prison. He remembered the last day.

"They give you some money and say goodbye. No bus ticket. My mom came and got me."

The young couple had met a year earlier, when Tiffany was recovering from a miscarriage.

"He was a jerk at first."

"I still had the prison mentality and she was glaring at me."

"I wasn't trying to stare."

"I said, 'If you have a problem with me come over and tell me, don't just glare at me.'"

I told them, it didn't sound like love at first sight.

"For me it was. For her I don't know."

They married in October 2008, two weeks after meeting. They lived in a trailer Tiffany owned on her mother's and stepfather's property. After the older couple split up, the van became home for Dan and Tiffany.

They saved $300 and moved to North Carolina for two months to help elderly relatives.

"I looked and there was no work down there. I applied at all the warehouses. I am a certified forklift operator. I have two years experience. They said, 'That ain't enough. We need four.' I said, 'You guys be smoking something.'"

Dan earns gas money catching feral cats and stray dogs for various animal protection groups.

"No one else has the guts to do it but me. They think I'm crazy."

Dan had a new plan. They would move near family who own a handyman service.

"I'm going to Missoula. I was thinking about going back East, but that is a lot of gas. I've got an aunt in Missoula. We don't want to live on the streets or in a camper anymore. They have a nice (homeless) shelter there and we're going to see if we can live in it."

Dan has two kids, younger than five, with his first wife.

"I'm not allowed to see them. I had to sign them over when I went to prison."

The couple claims the streets have changed.

"I see more homeless people than I have ever seen before," Dan said.

"Even the shelter is cracking down," Tiffany said. "You can stay at the living and family shelters, as a woman, for two to three months and then you have to leave for six weeks."

Apparently, Dan's self-admitted temper keeps them living in the van.

"They (employers) look at me like I'm a thief and a criminal and they better watch me twenty-four seven. I was working for a tire shop down there in Lodge Grass (Montana) and they changed the security codes and everything. I had to sit outside for twenty minutes waiting for someone to open the doors. And every time they put the code in they made me turn around, like I was a thief. I told them, 'You can take this job and shove it up your ass. I'm outta here. You are not going to treat me like this.'"

Tiffany's unemployment is chronic.

"I get a job, but I only last six months. I get bored with it. I guess that is part of the ADD. I have the attention span of a two-year-old child. I just kind of jump around. I've been in and out of the psych ward since I was sixteen."

Have they been tempted to do drugs?

"No way," said Dan. "Not after you've been in prison for two or three years. I have seen more stuff than anybody could ever see in their life. I've seen stuff that I'll never talk about."

The corpulent couple consented to a photo. The inside of their van was heaped with shabby mattresses, clothes and pulp fiction paperbacks. Evidence of their Walmart spree was everywhere; case after case of Top Ramen.

We said goodbyes. As they were leaving, Dan, then Tiffany, tossed popcorn on the pavement next to their van. Annoyed, I walked over to scoop it up and disgustedly found it wasn't popcorn at all. It was yesterday's Top Ramen. They simply tossed it, walked over it, jumped into their belching vehicle and then drove through it again. It served as a fitting metaphor for their troubled lives. Top Ramen had no meaning to them whatsoever. But it should have.

The couple still rumbles through my mind in a winsome "Bonnie and Clyde" way. Both seemed intelligent and could carry on engaging conversation. They didn't seem bitter and claimed to be drug-free. Who could know? I'll never see them again. Before they left, I asked Dan if he was angry at God for their circumstances.

"Hell no. It ain't God's fault that I am sitting here on the streets."

Tiffany was equally pragmatic.

"It's been a hard year, but we've battled through it. Sometimes a bump in the road comes along that helps you or throws you off balance. We are playing with the hand we were dealt. It's what you gotta do."

They vanished in a van with 400,000 miles on it.

****

John Steinbeck bought a hat in Billings. The GMC cap a friend gave me for Christmas was turning rather ratty after nine months daily use. I hit a Chevy dealer and a parts store to buy a GMC ball cap with red letters matching my truck's grille. No luck. At an actual GMC dealership, the parts department had not a single GMC ball cap and it would take days to "special order."

"Buddy," I told the counterman, "I'll be 500 miles gone by tomorrow."

****

My first Saturday night on the road was in Miles City, Montana. Steinbeck claimed to have gone to worship services every Sunday, but only mentioned the first. The church in Vermont featured a "fire and brimstone" preacher:

He put my sins in a new perspective. Whereas they had been small and mean and nasty and best forgotten, this minister gave them some size and bloom and dignity. I hadn't been thinking very well of myself for some years, but if my sins had this dimension there was some pride left. I wasn't a naughty child, but a first rate sinner, and I was going to catch it.

Saturday night I punched "churches" into my GPS. Narrowing my choices to two, neither seemed heaven-sent. Then, over the roofline of the Miles City Walmart, a white church spire soared. It was Baptist – the church of my youth. My decision had been made.

Next morning, the first man who greeted me in the sanctuary wore a suit and tie – he seemed older than the rest of the congregation. Most men were not in suits, but Montana-casual with cowboy hats, stiff shirts and rodeo boots.

"Are you a deacon or an elder?" I asked.

"Well no, I'm actually the pastor."

"Oops, sorry about that."

"No apologies needed. We don't have any airs around here. I've been in this town for thirty-five years. I'm from Kansas City. Here, I am a city slicker in cowboy country. Actually, my wife and I like it here. We'll stay as long as they will have us."

"I'm looking forward to the service."

"I try not to have too many sermons turn out to be clunkers. But every once in a while, one slips in. Hopefully, not today."

The pastor's message revolved around his belief that too many people simply fear God. He said forcefully that God is also love and forgiveness, using the Prodigal Son as his text.

He closed reading lyrics to *Tie a Yellow Ribbon Round the Old Oak Tree.* God is constantly tying yellow ribbons, the pastor said, welcoming us home. Forgiving those who stray.

"God is slow to anger, but quick to bless."

Later, in the church parking lot, a young man dragging on a cigarette was leaning on a new, decked-out Chevy pickup.

"Nice truck," I said.

"Thanks, but it only used to be nice."

He showed me a wrinkle across the tailgate that was punctured clear through.

"What year is it?" I asked.

"It's a 2009. That's why I'm so bummed. I just got it. It was my own damn fault."

"Grace never gives up," the pastor had said. Not sure how that registered to the young Montanan, his new Chevy truck suffering a puncture wound.

****

In the distance, 250 miles away, were the two graves of Sitting Bull. One in North Dakota. The other in South Dakota. Both were in shameful condition.

Farther still, a North Dakota town of fifty souls won the undying admiration of one of America's most notorious rock stars. The Dakotas had much to offer beyond amber waves of grain *down John's road.*

6   DAKOTA DAYS

What happens in Alice stays in Alice.

> Alice Cooper receiving
> The Key to Alice, North
> Dakota in 2006.

****

T wo hours after church ended in Miles City, I crossed from Montana into the Dakotas. John Steinbeck claimed to have visited the Badlands, but only mentioned visiting Beach, North Dakota – 240 miles from Badlands National Park. Steinbeck was in an area that looked like the Badlands and, I think, simply called them so.

For long stretches between Beach, Sentinel Butte and Medora, rock outcroppings jutted skyward with majestic concentric rings stacked one upon another.

Whatever the pediment's size, its pattern was repeated. Craggy rocks with slopes of finger-like fissures. Red grass or lichen about three-quarters of the way up topped with greenery: grass, small trees or bushes providing stark contrast to the brown, lifeless backdrop of the buttes. Over time, North Dakota winds must have blanketed each butte with fertile soil or sand. How else to explain lofty vegetation up so high?

In the central Dakota flatness, I lamented the sameness, the lack of scenery. Then outside Richardton, twin spires pierced the sky. They were part of a church or religious shrine. Startled by their size, I pulled off the Interstate to mingle among the streets and 577 residents of Richardton.

The spires were Assumption Abbey, "a place of worship and abode for Benedictine Monks on the prairie," said a brochure. Two women from Beach, North Dakota, walked into the cathedral before me and crossed themselves to pray. They told me Catholics from throughout North Dakota often make a yearly trek to the Abbey to do penance.

The monks who live on the grounds, sell wine for income, but also work as ranchers, teachers, pastors, chaplains, potters, scholars and writers. "However, seeking God in prayer is always at the center, our reason to exist," the brochure said.

A worship of another sort was going on in another part of town. Nothing was open except two taverns: Cheers & Beers featuring Miller Lite beer, while The Elkhorn Bar favored Pabst Blue Ribbon. Judging from vehicles parked outside, the Holy Grail of Sundays in America – the NFL – was holding services.

I hit the Interstate, passing up the opportunity nearby to see Salem Sue – World's Largest Holstein Cow.

****

A week into my trip, a great mystery arose – a tale of gravesites and birthplaces.

Cruising pool table flat I-90 outside Bismarck, I read my atlas. Near Selfridge, North Dakota, red letters announced "Sitting Bull Burial Site." Flipping to South Dakota, I was flummoxed to read "Sitting Bull's Grave" near Mobridge, South Dakota.

The North Dakota grave rested on the Standing Rock Indian Reservation. The South Dakota site reposed a half-hour away on a bluff over the Missouri River. How could revered Sitting Bull be buried in two places? Had they divided his ashes? Was there a dispute about his burial? Did locals truly not know and were simply guessing?

The journalist in me had to know. Sitting Bull had been one of the last Indian chiefs to acquiesce to the U.S. Army. After touring restlessly with Buffalo Bill's Wild West Show, Sitting Bull lived quietly in a cabin on South Dakota's Grand River. He groused about the white man's ways, had two wives and rejected Christianity.

A movement among young Indians called The Ghost

59

Dancers had reservation officials worrying Sitting Bull might embrace the fledgling attempt to restore tribal pride. Sitting Bull garnered such respect, officials wanted to divert or distract him. On December 15, 1890, Indian police approached his cabin in pre-dawn hours to detain him. The results were grim and bloody.

Whether Sitting Bull played a role in the mayhem is still debated. Shots rang out and bedlam ensued. Six tribal policemen were killed, as well as eight resisting Indians.

When the smoke settled, among the dead was Sitting Bull, shot in the torso and head. He was buried on the Standing Rock Indian Reservation near Fort Yates, North Dakota. In 1953, his remains were allegedly exhumed by relatives and moved to a more majestic overlook of the wide Missouri River near Mobridge, South Dakota. That site lies closer to his birthplace on the Grand River.

Both gravesites were unkempt during my mid-September visit. The Fort Yates site consisted of an unpaved parking lot, rock-filled road and patchy, brown lawn.

Meanwhile, two dumpsters surrounded the Mobridge site. At the base of a monument lay disjointed items: cigarette butt, penny, cheap cloth bracelet, feathers, open bottle of water, and Styrofoam dish filled with moldy cake.

Manure from range cattle or horses hardened in the midday sun. The site did not befit the chief whose warriors vanquished Lieutenant Colonel George Armstrong Custer at the Battle of Little Bighorn.

True dichotomy arose later on a farm ninety minutes away in Strasburg, North Dakota. Two miles down a gravel road, surrounded by a berm of trees, nestled a well-kept farmstead. Two volunteers tidied the grounds, washing screen windows apparently closing for the season. The grounds immaculate, the buildings housed a small museum. For five dollars, visitors received a short tour.

Music swirled from hidden speakers. An accordion-playing figurine poked from the loft of a barn. It was the birthplace of Lawrence Welk, Hungarian-American bandleader, famous in the 1960s for a Saturday night TV variety show.

That Welk, with his Euro-roots and musical kitsch should have his birthplace so well-funded seemed incongruous, when nearby reposed two Sitting Bull burial sites with no manicured lawns, no tidy buildings, and no volunteers to answer questions.

There was one tourist at the Sitting Bull and Welk sites. Me. With Labor Day over and kids in school, campgrounds, tourist sites and Sitting Bull's remains, wherever they were, hunkered down for winter.

Not so at two nearby casinos. By ten a.m., the Prairie Knights Casino and Pavilion had seventy-five vehicles. The Grand River Casino and Resort also showed signs of life.

Gaming thrived here, amid Lawrence Welk tinsel and the manure and moldy cake of Sitting Bull's many graves.

****

Heading east, the goal was Alice, North Dakota. Population: fifty. Still I hoped to find a good story. John

●●▶●●●●●▶●●●●●▶●●●●●▶●●●●●▶●●●●●▶●●●●●▶●●●●●▶●●

Steinbeck wrote about a picnic lunch in Alice near the Maple River. After too many Walmarts, with transient people in a hurry to anywhere else, I needed real people with real roots.

Alice nestled on a flat, agricultural plain. No stoplight. No stores. No neon-lit gas stations. Not even a U.S. Post Office. Churches looked unattended. A crew of steeplejacks was putting up a new communications tower for first-responders.

A man named Tim was out at his mailbox. The retired carpenter from Bemidji, Minnesota had lived in Alice for a decade and was taciturn, to say the least.

"I don't bother anyone and they don't bother me."

Struggling to find signs of life, I saw only a Little League baseball field.

"Does anything go on in this town, Tim?"

"Not much," he grunted. "If you want to know, go check that building. That's where the mayor works. I see his truck there."

It was a flat-roofed building like a 1960s schoolhouse. A sign proclaimed: *Nu-Tech Seed Company, North Dakota's Undisputed Round-up Ready, Soybean Yield Leader.*

Inside was tall, personable Dan Lund. Indeed, mayor of Alice.

"I'm the chief cook and bottle washer and roller upper of sidewalks."

"How long have you been mayor?"

"I suppose not quite twenty years. We used to have a seven-member city council, but we've slimmed it down to three."

In his day job as the regional sales manager for Nu-Tech,

62

Lund covers North Dakota, northern Minnesota and Montana with "seven or so" employees.

"Does that make you the leading employer in town?"

"That makes us the only employer in town," he quipped.

Raised in Nome, North Dakota, the mayor moved to Alice in 1988.

"What keeps you here?"

"Business. I started farming with my boy. I bought a house that I liked a lot. I liked it so much, I was going to move it out into the country. But we just stayed here in town. It's like living in the country. You can't get much better than this. It's quiet. Being mayor, I can keep everything under control."

Lund gave me a primer on Alice politics.

"Our whole budget is ... let's see. We chug along on about five grand a year. Our biggest expenditures are gravel, pushing some snow out and replacing streetlights. We have monthly meetings. It's a state law you know. We are a small town, but we run just like anybody else."

The mayor did not know John Steinbeck had mentioned Alice in *Travels with Charley.*

"I would have been in high school when he came through. I was probably reading one of his other books. Maybe *Of Mice and Men.*"

I asked the mayor what Steinbeck would have seen in 1960.

"The Interstate would have been open at that time. He might have gotten off thinking he was going to Buffalo seven miles north, or he could have come south to Alice. Or he might have been bumping along Highway 46, through

Enderlin and came up to here."

Is it probable Steinbeck saw more business in Alice than I did? Or so I lamented to the mayor.

"What's up with the empty storefronts?"

"We had a gas station. We used to have a bar/café and a grocery store. But they closed up about two years ago."

Pointing to the floor, Lund said, "This used to be an old school. They built it in 1962. It wouldn't have been here when (Steinbeck) came through. It was only open for four years. Then they closed it. The kids went to Enderlin. Then senior citizens used it as a meeting place. Then in 2001 they sold it to me because they were sorta dying off."

"I was able to almost create my own business. My range is out 200 miles. Soybeans and corn. That's what I do."

Soybeans and corn only go so far as a literature topic. I turned off my tape recorder. The mayor sensed my waning hopes of finding one noteworthy story about Alice. After I thanked him for his time and turned to leave, he played his ace card.

"Well, we do have one sort of claim to fame. About five years ago, we gave Alice Cooper the key to the city."

"You mean, the Alice Cooper? The rocker, the one who goes crazy on stage?"

"You can look it up on the Internet and you'll find references to it. We found out Alice was going to play Fargo, North Dakota. It was Mother's Day weekend. May 14, 2006."

"There was a guy on the city council that was a big Alice Cooper fan. He sent him an e-mail. He said, 'If you're coming through Fargo, we'd like to give you a key to the city.' Three months later he got in touch."

"Cooper said, 'Yah, shoot. That'd be cool.' So he came into Fargo on Saturday and he didn't play until Monday. He came out on Sunday afternoon. We had some bands out here, so we made a full day of it. Shoot, we had a couple thousand people."

"We should have called it The Alice Cooper Festival, but we weren't smart enough to give it an official name. You can look it up on Google and we're married to each other. You look up Alice Cooper and you get us. You look up Alice, North Dakota and you get Alice Cooper. It's crazy."

Lund told me Cooper was about sixty-one when he passed through, same age as Lund.

"He's got a lot more road miles on him though."

"We sent a limo in for him and it picked up a lot of press. When he pulled into town, he was escorted by the Highway Patrol. So I walked over to the patrolman, because usually they charge for that sort of thing. So I said, 'What about this expenditure?' And he said, 'There is no cost to you. I am retiring next week and I want him to sign my hat.' So Alice came in and signed his Smokey Bear hat."

"Cooper was very gracious. We set up a receiving line, so he wouldn't get mobbed by the people. Everybody that was standing there that wanted something signed, he gave them his autograph."

It was a good story from Lund and turned out be true. Sure enough, you can still find footage of Alice Cooper's 2006 visit on YouTube. Cooper, known for his stage presence, threw the Alice crowd a few one-liners.

"Has anybody been drinking today?" Cooper asked. "I had a feeling. What happens in Alice stays in Alice."

After a short acceptance speech, Cooper said: "When I come here I expect to pay for nothing. This is my town. I thought they were going to give me the whole town. I was going to sell it to (David) Bowie."

Mayor Lund said Cooper acted like an average guy.

"He did not put on make-up or act like a wild man. He did not sing or play. Those that rode out with him from Fargo said he was really cool to talk to. It's a case of his stage presence versus the real him."

According to Lund, there is no doubt Cooper put Alice on the map.

"It was the craziest thing. It must have been a slow news day. I got called by the AP for an interview. We got letters and e-mails from almost around the world. It made a paper in Norway. There was a kid working with the North Dakota Wheat Commission and I think he was working in Egypt. And he walks out and picks up his paper and there I was shaking hands with Alice Cooper."

Finally, I asked the mayor how the town got the name Alice.

Lund said the story goes that the Burlington and Northern Railway ran the train line through in 1900 and the surveyor had several daughters. So every seven miles there is a town: Mora, Alice, Katherine, Marion and Elizabeth.

"So they always called it 'The Ladies Line,'" Lund said.

Mayor Lund has not given up on a revival for Alice.

"There is a group of people trying to put together a convenience store, with a little café and gas station. Maybe a bar. Someplace to go. Right now we don't have a meeting place. We sort of miss that."

Climbing out of Lund's big truck, after a tour of Alice, I asked him how close his last election was.

"Some people wrote down Dan Lund. Two people wrote Buzzard Lund. And one person wrote Buzzard. So they said I got 10 votes. But the state said we have to register them exactly as they are written. So Dan Lund, Buzzard Lund, and Buzzard all came in first, second, and third on the first ballot. I was ten for ten. So I got a mandate."

"The time before I got eight votes and they wrote-in the bartender for two. I think that was kind of an inside deal. I think he bought some drinks."

How long is Lund going to serve?

"I think it's a lifelong deal."

I shook his hand and drove off. Suddenly, the mayor began waving wildly. Great, I thought, he's got another good story. No such luck. My collapsible steps attached to my camper were hanging off my tailgate and dragging noisily on the only road out of Alice, North Dakota. I was making sparks.

Thanks Mayor Lund. Now you really got my vote. Too bad I'll be long gone when the next election arrives.

****

Another town Steinbeck mentioned visiting was Detroit Lakes, Minnesota. So I stopped. Along picturesque East

Shore Drive were two forged historical plaques erected in 1996.

One of them had three typos permanently etched in the metal. *Building* was spelled *buliding*; *sight* was used where *site* should have been; there was a comma/quotation-mark juxtaposition. It was the old editor in me, but still The Becker County Historical Society and City of Detroit Lakes needed to hire better proofreaders.

The next morning I drove through Sauk Centre, Minnesota looking for Sinclair Lewis' birthplace as Steinbeck had in 1960. I saw an electrician taking a break in a local park.

"Can you tell me how to get to the Sinclair Lewis birthplace?"

"Yah, it's two streets over and down a bit. You can't miss it, a big sign out front."

"Can you tell me the name of the street?"

"Nah and I drive it every day. You'd think I'd know it by now."

"Do they commemorate Lewis every year?"

"You are looking at it. Right here in this park. They have a big festival. Lots of arts and crafts. Maybe some readings. It's a pretty big deal. It goes on for several days in July."

I found the Lewis home, but it was closed. A quick stop at the newspaper office flushed out Sinclair Lewis details.

The editor said the town hosted a writers conference every year, focusing on a Minnesota author or poet. The editor of *The Herald* was Bryan Zollman.

"I am a retired newspaper editor myself. I also edited a paper called *The Herald*."

"Retired? You still look pretty young to be retired. Maybe there is hope for me. The job doesn't kill you in the end."

****

As I left the upper Midwest, I noticed topographical and geographical changes. Mid-Minnesota made it final. I was fully surrounded by the emblems of farm country: corn, silos, and tractors.

In my salad days of youth, tractor brands were an item of pride. Farmall, Massey-Harris, Allis-Chalmers, Ford, Case, Oliver, and Minneapolis-Moline were a few.

In the agriculture I had seen on my trip thus far, only one tractor manufacturer ruled: John Deere. As the ad slogan proclaimed: *Nothing Runs Like A Deere.*

In the 1960s, a farmer had arrived if he owned a towering blue and white A.O. Smith Harvestore™ silo. They were a glass-lined status symbol in all widths and heights and considered a step above concrete or brick silos.

A.O. Smith began marketing Harvestore™ after World War II. An estimated 70,000 were sold in the Midwest over the next five decades. By the 1990s sales slowed for "Big Blue" as milk prices plummeted, family farms became an anachronism, and corporate farms with thousands of cows became the norm. Silage and hay are now stored in concrete bunkers or huge storage bags.

Harvestores™ still dot the countryside. Grass grows around their bases and the paint peels that once proclaimed the farmer's name (& sons) beneath a U.S. flag. The blue sentinels of the heartland, with white capstones, and implied success, remain a silent tribute to the family farm.

****

I raced on *down John's road* to a family wedding in the long shadow cast by Lambeau Field, Green Bay, Wisconsin. Afterward, a dying friend swore on his father's grave about the value of General Motors to an unappreciative America.

7   HOME IN THE HOMELAND

Weirdness is not my game. I'm just a
square boy from Wisconsin.

Actor Willem Dafoe.

****

In 1960, John Steinbeck was surprised by Wisconsin, enjoyed it immensely and called it among his favorite states – until he began an unabashed love affair with Montana, a thousand miles down the road:

I remembered now that I had been told Wisconsin is a
lovely state, but the telling had not prepared me. It was a

71

magic day. The land dripped with richness, the fat cows and pigs gleaming against green, and, in the smaller holdings, corn standing in little tents as corn should, and pumpkins all about.

In my big GMC truck on the Steinbeck road, I crossed into Wisconsin at Saint Croix Falls, the sun blazing brightly across kingdoms of tassel-topped corn. The tidiness of Wisconsin farms always amazes, even as the concept of family farms wanes. I have found no state where farmers are prouder of their acreage.

Freshly mowed lawns preened with straight lines and grids as if created by a Major League Baseball groundskeeper. Flower beds bloomed in weed-free bliss. Outdoor grills sat ever ready; bratwurst, beef, pork and chicken bound for Wisconsin waistlines.

Not infrequently, roadside tributes hail the Green Bay Packers. Sneering references to the Chicago Bears and Minnesota Vikings abound. In the fall, Wisconsin becomes a rolling football shrine with Packer windsocks, wind chimes, lawn ornaments and riding lawn mowers in war paint of green and gold. It has always been so since Vince Lombardi first coached in Green Bay in 1959, a year before Steinbeck's journey.

****

On my trip's twelfth day, I took part in a niece's al fresco country-western wedding in a cathedral of corn. Groomsmen wore work boots and western gear. Along rows of chairs were flowers stuffed into cowboy boots.

A horse-drawn wagon delivered the bride. The wedding rings came by pony. The pastor – a rough-hewn parson – spoke plainly, if not forcefully, about Samson and Delilah.

After the nuptials, guests were herded to a large shed for a Wisconsin hootenanny. Beer flowed. The bride tossed flowers, the groom his wife's garter. The DJ played Kenny Chesney music well into the night. *Roll Out The Barrel* – eternally a hit tune in Wisconsin – came after sunset as the hayride wagon circled.

Guests were asked to fill out cards with matrimonial advice. My job was to pick a few nuggets to read. Among the raunchy, borderline X-rated responses, came a few gems:

"Always eat a bowl of popcorn every week together."

"Birth control is for losers."

"Never sleep in a lumpy bed, or fart on a crowded bus."

The most repeated advice to the newly betrothed was the most timeless.

"Never let the sun go down on your anger."

"Keep the Lord in your marriage."

"The woman or bride is always right," or a counterpart, "Hey groom, do you want to be right, or do you want to be happy?"

It was a wedding to remember. No drunks, no rain, no gatecrashers. The groom began picking up chairs when the DJ music stopped. Someone reminded him he had better things to do.

••▶•••••▶•••••▶•••••▶•••••▶•••••▶•••••▶•••••▶••

****

Then I drove to a Milwaukee suburb to meet my high school basketball coach after forty years. He had led our team to unfathomable glory in the late 1960s. Two years running our teams were ranked No. 1 among small Wisconsin schools and played in jam-packed gyms, with below zero temperatures outside.

He didn't coach after leaving my hometown in the early 1970s, preferring guidance counseling. He is a private and reserved man. We enjoyed three hours together over lunch at a sports bar restaurant.

I told him how in Senior English in 1970, he had introduced me to John Steinbeck. On his required reading list was *The Red Pony*. Coach did not remember much about teaching English Literature, claiming he felt several students had been smarter on the topic than he was.

However, he had no equal as a basketball coach. He could recall with perfect clarity many sweet victories, and fortunately, only a few galling defeats on the hardwood.

"I think about it all the time," Coach said.

****

Leaving Milwaukee's suburbs, I had to backtrack through Wisconsin Dells, a place Steinbeck churned through in 1960. In twilight, I rolled through Wisconsin's top tourist attraction. The Dells remains a colorfully contrived place, a destination spot for Midwesterners since the late 1800s.

●●▶●●●●●▶●●●●●▶●●●●●▶●●●●●▶●●●●●▶●●●●●▶●●●●●▶●●

Built first around sandstone cliffs of the Dells along the Wisconsin River, the city of 2,500 now calls itself "The Water Park Capital of the World." Theme parks dot the intersections and hotels have great water tunnels that flow out of upper levels like emergency chutes from airplanes.

But on this mid-September night, the Dells had begun shutting down. What is more forlorn than a water theme park – without water? I could only imagine kids and teenagers screaming as thousands of gallons of water and gravity jetted them to slippery landings.

In Wisconsin for nearly a week, I had not yet visited my hometown of Evansville. The constant urge to move to Illinois for the slow trek east would have to wait.

When Steinbeck arrived in his native Salinas in 1960, "the fight began." Steinbeck argued unendingly with his sisters. They had remained Republicans more or less. The policies of JFK, RFK, and LBJ were fertile debate ground. The brickbats passed between siblings were tiring, at fever pitch for the duration of his visit.

My family has remained fairly Republican and we rarely argued politics. Even so, I spent one uncomfortable evening with my older sister. Evening traipsed into morning. Hurtful words exchanged. Words only siblings of six decades would dare sling.

The dust-up wasn't about Obama or Tea Party politics. Instead we slung the darts and arrows of family matters.

It was not one of the trip's shining moments. It is the one night of eighty I would like a do-over. Real life doesn't allow instant replays.

●●▶●●●●●▶●●●●●▶●●●●●▶●●●●●▶●●●●●▶●●●●●▶●●●●●▶●●

****

Swaying in a gentle autumn breeze were thousands of acres of corn surrounding my hometown. Locals told me for a week that "we didn't really have a summer around here." No one told that to the corn. It was a farmer's pride at nine feet tall in places.

One day I drove around the town of my youth. The memories are there. The roads are there. Schools you attended and old stores and factories are there. The local newspaper and mailbox stencils reveal familiar names.

You can go past the *house* you grew up in, but your *home* is gone. To that degree, you cannot go home again.

Small Midwestern towns, if they are growing, move to the edges. What used to be my hometown A & W root beer stand, serving families and employing teens, was now the Police Department. What used to be a Dairy Queen morphed into an Italian restaurant.

A peek inside an old bowling alley I used to frequent proved disillusioning. It was where I spent a chunk of my early twenties trying to understand the ways of alcohol and girls – not proving very good at either.

The ownership and layout had changed in three decades. It felt like a hovel, dank, and full of shadows. There was the smell of hamburgers and pizza. A gaggle of young people surrounded a long bar this Saturday afternoon. In this familiar place, there was not a single familiar face. With my memory painfully losing focus, I fled.

Four miles west of town sits the small farm where I grew

up. Only the aging farmhouse and small outbuildings remain. The main barn and sheds were long ago consumed by fire.

My father's eighty-acre farm sat nearly unrecognizable. It had been subdivided. Its hills were dotted with large, stately haciendas on hills I used to sled as a child.

No vehicles were seen in the driveway, or I would have asked to look around. Driving back to town, by accident I met an old friend of decades past. In demeanor and mannerism he remained the same. The chuckle in his voice and even the way he tucked his fingers under his suspender overalls were still familiar.

We told a few stories of playing pick-up baseball on front lawns with trees as first, second and third base. We talked of harsh winter storms and impassable roads.

Eventually, he pointed out farms on the near and distant horizon still owned by the farmers we had known fifty years ago. There weren't many. He told me of one local family making a go milking just sixty cows – a concept I believed long dead.

Later in my visit, I met a dying friend. His name was Russ and he was in later stages of melanoma, but taking part in medicine trials at a local university. His outlook was not good.

We joined another old friend and went to a baseball game in Milwaukee. On the way back, the dying friend felt the need to vigorously defend his three-decade career at a recently shuttered General Motors assembly plant.

"I'm sick and tired of these Congressmen sitting up there and asking questions of all the motor executives like they know what they are talking about. They don't. They have some aide talking in their ear."

"I'm proud of my GMC career, damn proud. I will not apologize for it. Did GM do some stupid things? Yes. Did those GMC executives give the unions everything they asked for? Sure. Should they have, on some of those occasions? Probably not."

"They bought a lot of companies they shouldn't have. They were running GMC like the federal government. The only trouble is the government can print money. GMC was pretty powerful, but they weren't that powerful. They couldn't print money."

"I saw some dumb stuff. I saw some management mistakes for sure. Was this the only plant they mismanaged? Probably not. I'm not stupid."

"People just run their mouth off when they don't know anything about how GMC works. They just quote numbers and they are always wrong."

"General Motors and those of us who worked there were such easy and big targets. And I'm sick and tired of being a target. I've got a year to live and I'm not going to take it anymore. I'm proud of every day I worked there. To anybody who wants to badmouth GMC, I say one thing: f_ _ _ you."

Saying goodbye to my dying friend, hoping I would see him again, another friend recommended I take Russ along for several weeks. Russ studied the possibility for awhile, but eventually rejected the notion. He wanted to stay near doctors and experimental medicines.

Doctors told him his melanoma had moved to his liver and

●●▶●●●●●●▶●●●●●▶●●●●●▶●●●●●▶●●●●●▶●●●●●▶●●●●●▶●●

would soon move to his brain or other soft tissue.

Russ was going through his house, designating certain items for brothers, sisters and friends. He had never married and had no children.

To his oncologist, Russ had demonstrated a deserved anger toward the cancer. The doctor recommended a psychologist. Russ resisted for months, finally relenting under the doctor's pressure.

In days, the psychologist sent back a report to the oncologist. Russ was not clinically depressed, suicidal, or in need of any serious counseling or medication. He was just mad at dying.

"Who could fault you for that?" Russ said. "There ain't no pill to knock that out, is there?"

Russ had lapsed in his Catholic faith and I asked him if he was angry at God for the apparent shortened lifespan. His own father had died at a young age leaving a grieving widow and many siblings. Russ' father had also worked at General Motors.

"I don't know about God. I just don't know. I went to church until I was thirty-nine years old, and then I just couldn't see it anymore. My mom talked me into going again after I got my diagnosis, but I just couldn't do it. I just don't know how you can guarantee God is going to be waiting for you when you die. How do you know? Maybe religion is just a big bluff. I don't know."

Trying to ease Russ' mind a little, I told him I still believed in God, though at times I was angry. This was one of those times. Why, for instance, did my wife have to suffer so under her now apparently permanent brain injury? She was just starting a career as a nurse. She trained so hard. Then it was yanked away. Why, why, why?

"When I get to the Pearly Gates, Russ, I'm going to be pissed as well. I'm going to have some questions, tough questions, in-your-face questions to ask God."

"He'll just send you to a psychologist," Russ roared with laughter.

****

Later, I learned Russ had died May 2, 2010, losing a 12-round, heavyweight fight to his cancer. He vowed never to check into a hospital – afraid he would never leave. That turned out true.

He had needed a procedure to relieve stomach pressure and was checked into a Madison, Wisconsin hospital and died two days later. He was off to see if God really stationed psychologists at the Pearly Gates.

****

As Steinbeck left Salinas in 1960, he drove to the highest peak for a last look. Fremont Peak soared much higher and more majestic over Salinas than modest Magnolia Bluff over southern Wisconsin near Evansville. I drove up anyway.

A storm was approaching and cast ominous shaded light over the cornfields. The view had not changed in forty years since my family picnicked there. Hay fields were trimmed close after multiple cuttings. New in the frame were the fast-ripening soybean fields. Green pods were turning yellow. My hometown's sign bragged: *Soybean Capital of Wisconsin.*

Chased into town by the storm, I drove over a half-mile section of Main Street recently resurfaced with brick pavers. They rumbled deeply, resonating unevenly through the truck and into my body. I too was beginning to feel uneven on the trip; an undefined soul ache slowly creeping in.

Unlike Steinbeck, I hold no bitterness toward my hometown and return there often. Yet, a certain dreariness descended as I left on a late Sunday afternoon. Rain, rare on my trip, did not help.

****

The days ahead would ebb and flow *down John's road.* Somewhere in Michigan a pastor polished a sermon that implored your best friend might be a person in hell. But the only hell I uncovered in the next week was the worst omelet ever served to mankind.

8   PEWS AND COMBINES

Life is fatal, futile and final.

Pastor in Hillsdale, Michigan.

****

The big GMC truck and Wolverine Camper plodded through the Midwest; John Steinbeck in 1960, I in 2009. Steinbeck's impressions, recorded in *Travels with Charley*, could have been my own today. He was most impressed with the increase in population and the "fluid energy" of Midwesterners.

Coming from the west in 2009, the masses first hit me gradually in Minnesota and Wisconsin, then fully in Illinois.

●●▶●●●●●●▶●●●●●●▶●●●●●●▶●●●●●●▶●●●●●●▶●●●●●●▶●●●●●●▶●●

From Seattle to Chicago, I had only flirted with Spokane, the Twin Cities and Milwaukee. Chicago's big shoulders and bigger freeways could not be avoided.

On September 20, I crossed the Wisconsin-Illinois state line, probably the first such boundary I ever crossed at age two. Later in the mid-1960s, I traveled to Wrigley Field often to watch the Cubs of Ernie Banks, Ron Santo, Billy Williams and Ferguson Jenkins.

Baseball was not on my mind this day. Instead, I was thinking about the upscale Ambassador East Hotel.

One morning in Woodstock, Illinois began in difficulty. Anxiety gripped me as I thought about driving into Chicago. I scooted only an hour closer to my destination. Fifty miles was ridiculous compared to prior daily averages. Not exactly was I taking Chicago by storm.

My wife called. Things were not well at home. She was stymied at every turn. Her brain injury symptoms were worsening; my own issues seemed innocuous. Once, I even threatened to end the trip and turn toward home. That pushed my wife too far. She would not hear it.

"We'll talk in the morning," she said and hung up. The clear message? Get a grip.

The next morning I awoke to airplanes flaring in and out of O'Hare International Airport. A sense of duty drove me to slip onto Chicago's Illinois Tollway. The Ambassador East Hotel was perhaps twenty miles away. In that distance, sense and sensibility returned. A road renaissance occurred.

Gabilan moved confidently amid the throbbing thruways of the Windy City. My truck lurched forward as if pulled by mechanical horses. Led by GPS, linked to a satellite miles overhead, soon I was in the Gold Coast of North Chicago. Children tethered by ropes and sporting bright blue safety vests moved from pre-schools into nearby Lincoln Park.

Tight streets, embroidered with taxis, moving vans, delivery trucks, and postal vehicles moved Chicago's commerce. Finding the Ambassador East proved easy, but a parking spot was an illusion. My plan was to park, laze in the famous Pump Room, drink coffee, snag pastries, and head to Indiana.

Steinbeck himself had to gird his loins to get from Chicago's suburbs to the Ambassador East. Steinbeck panicked in big city traffic, so he started into the city before daylight, still got lost, and had a taxi driver lead him to the grand hotel.

With a GPS on my dashboard, I didn't need a taxi to find the swanky hotel. Driving laps around the Ambassador East, the elegant doorman stared at the rig. When Steinbeck pulled up in 1960, he jauntily flipped the keys to the doorman and said he'd be back in a week.

Steinbeck was well known around the establishment. If I had flipped my keys to the doorman, I might never have seen Gabilan again. I was a stranger among strangers. Steinbeck, however rumpled, was in his element:

I think I am well and favorably known at the Ambassador East, but this need not apply when I arrive in wrinkled hunting clothes, unshaven and lightly crusted with the dirt of travel and bleary-eyed from driving most of the night.

Simply stopping under the Ambassador East's regal portico would have been an act of supreme chutzpah. Increasing my range to four or five blocks from the Ambassador East, there was still no logical spot to park. Snickering at myself for putting on a clean pair of slacks and a collared shirt for my grand Pump Room appearance, I drew no closer to The Pump Room than to The Oval Office.

Finally, I summoned courage to pull squarely in front. A snappy, curious, concierge approached.

"Can I help you sir," he said, pulling at his wrist-high white gloves.

"One photo. That's all I want. It's important to me."

"Surely sir. No problem."

He took my digital camera and walked into the narrow street as taxis and a limo waited. Oblivious, I leaned against my truck as the man clicked away.

"Nice rig," a man in business suit said.

I gave him a quick thank you, and pondered the last time any businessman, curbside at the Ambassador East, had seen a hulking GMC truck pull up with camper aboard.

Grateful to the concierge, I drove away from a most pleasurable moment.

Looking at the photo later, my pride seems to ooze from me as I stood in front of the grand hotel. I crossed my arms in khaki pants and wriggled my walrus mustache like Hemingway returning from safari.

That moment was likely as close as I am ever to get to the Ambassador East. Its famous Pump Room remains virgin

territory to me, proclaimed by a Web site as "Historic
Grandeur on Chicago's Gold Coast":

*Still the place to be seen, its regal stature firmly in place,
the eminent Ambassador East Hotel has been a magnet to
distinguished guests such as Frank Sinatra, Richard Gere,
Gary Sinise and Vince Vaughn.*

Robert Redford and Paul Newman ate lunch there daily,
dining on ham sandwiches and drinking pilsner beer during
filming of *The Sting*. No mention of John Steinbeck – the
nerve of the place to forget him.

Leaving for a quick glimpse of Wrigley Field, in true
Steinbeck mimic, I got lost. My GPS had fallen to the floor,
unreachable in midday traffic. Trolling south on Lake Shore
Drive, I paid homage to the John Hancock Building, Navy
Pier, Soldier Field, and sprawling Grant Park where Barack
Obama had proclaimed victory eleven months before.

Eventually I settled for the Interstate and Knute Rockne
Travel Plaza in Indiana with Dairy Queen and McDonald's –
a sad sniff compared to the Ambassador East's Porcina
Risotto, Beef Tartare, and Ricotta Gnocchi.

****

As I skirted Gary and Hammond, Indiana, acres of slag
heaps and refinery farms dotted the land. Three weeks and a
day on the road, a milestone appeared: my first Greyhound
bus of the entire journey. Surely Steinbeck saw more in 1960.

●●▶●●●●●▶●●●●●▶●●●●●▶●●●●●▶●●●●●▶●●●●●▶●●●●●▶●●

I headed to Amish country. Many Amish and Mennonites use tractors now, though they go to town for supplies behind horse and buggy. Young men were coming home from work laboring stroke by stroke on bikes. Most had straw hats, and many wore beards – a riddle I would solve later.

****

In Angola, Indiana, I did not have a plan; the first day of the entire trip that I had no end destination.

Breakfast became the plan. The restaurant I chose had "family" on the billboard, a full parking lot, and an overly friendly waitress who plunked a huge menu before me.

Spying the Farmer's Omelet, I asked the waitress, "What's in it?"

"Everything the cook can find in the kitchen."

That should have been a hint. The omelet was a tasteless mishmash of runny eggs, mystery meat, flaccid vegetables and spices leftover from the Mayflower's journey. For eight dollars and ninety-five cents, its only redeeming value was its hugeness. I made it one-third through before throwing a culinary penalty flag.

Many U.S. prisons today serve The Loaf – leftovers, any leftovers, compressed from the day before. Judges, reacting to inmate lawsuits, have ruled as long as the food is not stale or rancid, it goes on the tray. This day in Indiana, I knew why prisoners rebel against something that is food *in name only*.

Moving to the hash browns, I sought sustenance, but found flatulence-inducing spuds instead. The hash browns were hashed, but not brown. They glistened with grease.

Surely, the side order of pancakes would save the day. But when they arrived with powdered sugar on top, the concept was lost. If I would have wanted a small first snowfall of confectioner's sugar, I'd have ordered it.

The pancakes flaked off like a calving glacier. The consistency was cornbread – three days old. Instead of calories clinging to each other, I imagined them repelling from the dreadfulness. Truly it was an abhorrent meal in America's Heartland.

Normally, I am an easy customer. Waitresses and cooks need not fear me. Not this day in Angola, Indiana. As reverse testament, I never again ordered a full breakfast the entire trip.

****

The day improved, it had to. Angling toward Gladwin, Michigan where my camper had been built, I needed certain interior adjustments to allow the 10,000-mile journey to continue. Not due in central Michigan for three days, I had time and distance to kill.

A red tractor saved me. Outside Jonesville, Michigan, I watched an elderly man maneuver an antique Farmall onto a trailer.

"Are you going to a tractor show?"

"No, I'm headed to the county fair over in Hillsdale."

"Really? When does it start?"

"Sunday. There's a big parade on Monday."

A sucker for a county fair, I programmed Hillsdale into my GPS. Outside Chicago, I was whisker-close to ending the trip, but a county fair in a college town brought rejuvenation. In Hillsdale, at day's end, I checked out the fairgrounds. It was a throwback from my youth. Every August in the 1960s, my family attended a county fair – the last bookend of summer.

Final fair preparations were ongoing. Tractor dealers were polishing four-wheel drive behemoths – one had a sticker price of a quarter-million dollars.

Midway roustabouts were tightening screws and bolts, cigarettes lolling from lips, T-shirts revealing tan skin, bulging biceps and obligatory tattoos. A wooden grandstand promised races or concerts.

I vowed to return on Sunday – opening day.

****

Hillsdale College was nearby; a pristine landscape. Rustling leaves did so in orderly fashion. A twisting cobblestone path featured inlaid bricks from alumni. Some messages were in Latin and referred to teachers or Bible verses. One caught my eye: *He who wanders is not lost.* It was a derivation of a line by J.R.R. Tolkien.

Statues of Lincoln, Jefferson, Washington and Margaret Thatcher dotted the campus, each festooned with a conservative message.

The next day, in a bowling alley bar, I watched my alma mater play college football on TV and drank too much beer.

In a Saturday afternoon daze, I slept it off in my rig in the parking lot. Later, out walking, I felt like a zombie my head hurt so badly. I skulked around town looking for the next day's church service. I needed penance.

Sunday proved a revelation. At sunrise, the wind blew gently. I found a Free Methodist Church and it was packed. The preacher was a visiting district superintendent – a small man with a soothing voice. A message board promised "A Message from the Grave."

The text was Luke 16, the tale of a rich man who ends up in hell, while the beggar Lazarus rises to heaven to sit beside Abraham. The rich man begs Abraham to allow Lazarus to dip his finger in water to come relieve his fiery agony in Hades. Abraham refuses, saying the chasm between heaven and the man's thirst is eternal.

The rich man pleads from Luke 16, verses 27-28:

"... Then I beg you, father, send Lazarus to my father's house, for I have five brothers. Let him warn them, so that they will not also come to this place of torment."

The pastor's point? "Life is fatal, futile, and final." There are no answers and no relief for those who beg after death. His deeper point was, how do we know this? From the story of Lazarus, the rich man and Abraham – that was the message from the grave.

With that theology to unravel, I was off to Americana itself – a county fair. Like a magnet, I found the tractor exhibit first. There I met Leon Beaubien and his joy – a pristine red and yellow Massey Harris tractor. Painted brightly, its tires polished to an ebony sheen.

He was from Hudson, Michigan. His tractor was a model E33.

"This tractor is a 1955 model. I bought it in 1957 after coming home from the Army."

"How much you pay for it?"

"I never answer those kinds of questions directly."

Leon sold it after he and his father quit farming in 1959.

"But I kept my eye on that tractor. The man I sold it to died in 2000. I bought it back in 2002. ... I'd take $5,000 for it now. Not that anyone would offer that."

Leon reached for a bag of Mail Pouch tobacco and gently placed a plug under his lip.

"I don't want nothing sweet," he slobbered through speckled lips.

****

The midway offered food for a trencherman: hand-rolled pretzels, hand-dipped corn dogs, hand-made onion rings. These were complemented by elephant ears, cheese on a stick, mozzarella fingers, giant breaded pork tenderloin sandwiches, sausage (Polish or Italian) and chips. To finish the culinary parade were toasted almonds and deep-fried ice cream.

Surely enough damage is done to the arteries of Hillsdale County residents during fair week to keep cardiologists and heart surgeons busy for decades.

While adults feasted, kids and teens whizzed on midway monsters named Sling Shot, Cliff Hanger, Freak Out, Tilt-A-

Whirl, Sizzler, and The Skater.

Walking through the animal barns, I scratched a horse called Hokey Pokey, a calf named Rosey, and a heifer called Elymay. My personal line was drawn at scratching a pig's ear.

The last act was a "Combine Demolition Derby." The grandstand was packed with gawkers paying eight dollars to see rigs destroy each other instead of rows of maize and grain.

A series of elimination rounds saw sparks fly, dirt spew, and kids scream as announcers egged on the general mayhem.

It became obvious each rig had an Achilles' heel. A death blow could be landed on tiny rear tires that immobilized the mechanical mastodons. Much as protecting radiators in an automobile demo derby is critical, keeping your rear tires out of harm's way was a ticket to fame for combine cowboys.

A puny John Deere combine, no beauty to look at, played the waiting game, squirting and darting as bigger rigs devoured each other. The little John Deere won the trophy as the crowd roared.

It was unbelievable fun. If John Steinbeck had been sitting beside me, I'm convinced he would have roared in glee. Thomas said his father loved to tinker with mechanical things. I think he would have appreciated the metal smashing between heats as owners coaxed battered combines into the ring one last time.

And the winner proved a John Deere – about as American as it gets *down John's road.*

****

There would be more Amish in coming days – up close and personal. An Amish couple told the unbelievable story of driving an aging Cadillac to Las Vegas and back – back to the faith of their fathers and mothers.

●●➤●●●●●➤●●●●●➤●●●●●➤●●●●●➤●●●●●➤●●●●●➤●●

9   THE AMISH

I am who I am. There are no secrets around here.

Dan Schwartz,
Amish husband, father.

****

The third week of September I hit Amish country.
Serendipity came in Shipshewana, Indiana, a town of
536 people and the only Indiana location in the
original best-seller *1,000 Places to Visit Before You Die.*

Of dozens of Amish-centric towns, I chose Shipshewana,
named for a Potawatomi Indian Chief whose nomadic tribe
settled the area. They were eventually force-marched to

Kansas in 1838 at a cost of three-dozen lives. Kansas was not for the chief. By 1839 he returned to Indiana where he died in 1841, about when Amish and Mennonites moved to Indiana from Pennsylvania. They never left. Moseying through northeast Indiana, I learned about the Swiss Anabaptist movement of 200 years ago that later became Amish and Mennonite culture.

Non-Amish people are called "English" in northern Indiana. Shipshewana had fewer *English* than Amish/Mennonite, making it perfect for mingling with bearded farmers, their bonneted wives, and obedient children.

Outside town, I passed a buggy with two barefoot boys snacking on bag candy – I think it was M&Ms. I waved at most buggy drivers; a few waved back with studied caution.

In Shipshewana, I maneuvered through mounds of horse manure like a student driver on a pylon course. Behind a general store, I parked near a buggy in which a young Amish father and his two children were waiting.

"Mind if I take a picture of your buggy?"

"Go right ahead."

"How about a photo of your rig and my truck?"

"Be my guest."

"I'm traveling the country and it'll be a neat photo next to an Amish rig. You are Amish, aren't you?"

"What else?"

"You sure have a handsome horse."

"That's Arnie the trotter. He's got it easy. I must say, you've got a pretty nice horse there yourself," the Amish man said pointing to my GMC rig.

I asked him if he had ever driven a car?

"Yah, fifteen years ago when my wife and I took a trip out West. Only she wasn't my wife then."

"Were you on Rumspringa?"

"That's right. So you know about Rumspringa?"

Admitting to being an Amish aficionado, I knew Rumspringa means "running around" in Pennsylvania-Dutch – the principal Amish tongue. Young adults are allowed to stray from Amish ways for however long it takes to go *English* or re-embrace parental ways and get baptized into the faith.

"Rumspringa is not forced on you, it just kind of happens. Every generation does it," the man said.

We shook hands firmly. His name was Dan Schwartz. Dan's demure wife Lena had finished shopping and climbed into the buggy. Dan was bemused by my rapid-fire questions. Without moving a muscle, Dan stared with piercing blue eyes. He wore a perfectly starched, collared white shirt. His leather shoes shined brightly. His wife or children rarely spoke. The encounter had a distinct serenity. My questions kept coming.

"Why are you in town?"

"My wife needed groceries. We come to town once a week or so."

I asked Dan why some men had beards and others not?

"You grow the beard once you get married."

"So it's kind of an off-limits sign to other women?"

"I suppose you could say that, but that's not how we would view it."

"How about an airplane? Ever been on one?"

"Airplane travel is frowned on, but you can in an emergency."

The questioned became questioner. Dan asked why I was in Shipshewana. In 100 words, I told him about Steinbeck's journey and my re-enactment.

"Have you ever heard of John Steinbeck?"

"I suppose I should have. Books were never my thing in school. I should have listened better I guess. I pretty much stick to the Bible these days."

"Well if you only read one book, I guess that'd be the one."

Raindrops caused steam to rise off Arnie's back and flanks and spattered off the buggy's metal black rims.

"They never go flat, that's for sure," Dan said.

Dan grabbed the reins. I thanked them for their time and asked for an address.

"If you want to get in touch again, you can just call us."

"You have a telephone?"

"Well not really in the house. It's down by the driveway. We use it as kind of an answering service."

They gave me their number and my questions grew bolder.

"Do you have a computer or access to the Internet?"

"No, we haven't gone that far yet. Probably won't."

"Did you vote for President Obama last fall?"

"No, we'd rather pray for him."

They drove off to their ten-acre farm, three miles outside town.

As I drove through Indiana and Michigan in coming days, the family stuck in my mind. I had to return to Shipshewana to see their farm, ask more questions. I called the number which rang in a box at the end of the driveway. I left a message. Minutes later, Dan called and we arranged my return for several days later.

****

Arriving on a bright Saturday afternoon, the small Schwartz farm was among the neatest in a universe of orderly farms. The lawn was immaculate, ready for Tiger Woods, I joked.

Corn shocks were propped on the front steps; an altar to autumn. We talked in their living room for several hours. The home was simple, spartan, but splendidly appointed. When I brought out my tape recorder, Dan grew nervous.

"I would prefer you not use that machine. The tape recorder would make me a little uncomfortable."

"Fair enough."

The parents and four children sat comfortably. Dallas was thirteen, Jenny eleven, Titus seven and Lindsey three. Their politeness seemed natural, not schooled. The kids probably wished they were elsewhere, but answered my questions, if a bit shyly. Dan and Lena added editorial comment if an answer strayed. Titus played an NFL Game Boy and nearby purred Kobe, a cat named after NBA star Kobe Bryant.

The NFL? The NBA? A telephone? The professional lawn? It bothered me and I asked.

"It all seems like the rest of us *English*. How is it all decided? How does technology and American culture seep into Amish families?"

"A lot of progress just creeps up on you," Dan said. "A little here. A change there. You know we do have our guidelines. But the next thing you know, the change is there and no one really remembers how it came about. For instance, I never had a phone growing up. We always went to the neighbors. It got to a point where you thought you might be kind of intruding. Maybe it became a nuisance."

"So now, as your own head of household, you decided to have a phone?"

"Yes, but it will never be in the house. That would be an intrusion. Might be a little too tempting."

Lena's hometown is Sugarcreek, Ohio near Canton. Her large family had three sisters and five brothers. Lena said half are non-Amish, either Mennonite or *English*.

"But we do not care what our culture may be," Dan said. "We are still one happy, God-fearing family, just trying our best to be ambassadors for Christ. We are here on this earth only for a short time. We believe in 'J-O-Y.'"

Dan explained: *J*esus first. *O*thers second. *Y*ourself last.

Born in nearby LaGrange, Indiana, Dan's family was even larger with three sisters and nine brothers. Two of his brothers are on Rumspringa as carpenters in Florida.

"Will they return to Amish ways?"

"We just hope and pray someday they will become born-again people and join some kind of a Christian church. God works in mysterious ways. You know what they say."

If they return, most young Amish marry by age twenty-two or so. Lena said marriage is a rite of passage into the essence of Amish faith.

"We have to prove to them (church elders) that you are more than just interested. You have to prove you are serious," she said.

An engaged couple attends nine counseling sessions, followed by baptism, and only then, marriage.

"You get to that point of time in your life, where you are ready to settle down," Dan said. "To put all that other stuff behind you. It is not all about myself. There is a reason for this life. God wants to be a part of this. Jesus came for our salvation. He will forgive our sins if we just ask him for forgiveness."

Christianity is integral to the Amish, but there are no churches. Services rotate between homes. Dan and Lena host once a year. Services last for hours and Dallas said a lot of teenage boys doze off.

"Some of the boys might fall asleep," Dan frowned. "But I think Dallas might be exaggerating a little bit. Church is a good thing."

Church starts promptly at nine a.m. and can last three hours.

"It varies. There are actually no real breaks, but we do all rise and stand when the preacher reads a chapter out of the Bible. That's when we go to the bathroom, if we need to."

There are forty-four families in Dan and Lena's congregation, run by an elected bishop, two ministers and one deacon.

"If a church gets too big, they will divide it in two. That happens now and then again."

Amish children in Shipshewana speak a form of German and English called Pennsylvania Dutch. They go to school until eighth grade and ride a bus to school where fifty percent of the students are Amish.

I asked Dallas if he wanted to be an astronaut or his sister a nurse, would they be allowed to go on in school. Dallas, a wide-shouldered, handsome boy, warily eyed his father across the room.

"We would frown on that," said Dan, "although there have been exceptions."

The family reads the local daily *The Goshen News*. When? Who knows?

The couple gets up at three thirty a.m. Dan must be ready for his commute to nearby Bristol, Indiana where he begins work at five a.m. for a high-end RV manufacturer. He rides in the vehicles of co-workers.

While Dan troubleshoots $500,000 plus RVs, Lena works at home using a gas-powered generator for laundry, sewing, and ironing. The stove and reefer are run by LP gas – no electricity lines led to their pristine property.

The children were asked for their favorite meal. The unanimous answer was homemade pizza.

"Yes, I have frozen foods, but on Monday I try and prepare a meal from scratch," Lena said.

"She is an excellent cook," Dan said. "You need to swing by sometime and try her Chicken Alfredo and Italian salad."

The couple uses a bank debit card. They do not have health

insurance per se. Jenny contracted leukemia at age three, taking chemotherapy for more than two years.

"We, as church members, have a free-will plan. When someone has a hospital bill, all surrounding churches chip in."

The day and interview drew long. During a quick tour of the property, Storm the pony, Kobe the cat, and Cliff the dog were introduced.

The carriage room was immaculate and the buggy proved state-of-the-art. One of Dan's brothers built it; a top-end buggy costs up to $8,000. The Schwartz' ride was definitely top notch. It had a heater, extra LED lights, thermo-pane windows, courtesy lights, armrests and flip-down seat. Titus ran his fingers carefully over the rudimentary dashboard, much as any youngster might over his father's new Chevy Malibu.

A good horse costs $3,000. Arnie was definitely "a good horse." Dan said hay was very expensive as well. Adding the carriage price, horse and hay, you arrive at the cost of a Honda Civic or Toyota Corolla. But there were no car dealerships visible in Shipshewana – only one of the largest horse auctions in the Midwest.

Had Dallas driven Arnie and the rig to town yet?

"Nope, he'd rather ride his bike," his father said.

We ambled toward my truck. Time to go. But not before one final kudo on the perfect lawn.

"That's Lena. Her thing is mowing the lawn. That's her away time. Quiet time. It's more than just the exercise. It's where she does her thinking."

My two visits with the Amish family were over. Would I ever see them again? If I wrote honestly about them in my book, would they want to see me again?

Just talking to me placed them in a kind of jeopardy. Amish are usually publicity shy, if not averse. Many won't allow photos. To be interviewed for a book, in more conservative Amish communities, might put tongues to wagging.

As the family walked away, I wanted Dan to understand I appreciated his courage.

"Not all your Amish brothers and sisters would have allowed me photos like you did last week behind Yoder's General Store. And I know many of them would not sit down with a perfect stranger with a pen and notebook in hand. I appreciate it. I really do."

Dan gripped my hand firmly, his blue eyes piercing deeply.

"I am who I am. There are no secrets around here."

****

For days my thoughts swirled about this family and the dichotomy of their lives.

Were they bearded men with no health insurance, wives with bonnets and children riding bikes to town? Was it life devoted to church along with forty-four other families, among whom there would be no secrets? Was it a home with no power lines, television, or computers, where no one votes or joins the military? Was it having a child with leukemia, trusting neighbors to defray staggering medical bills?

Or was it the other?

A young boy playing an NFL Game Boy, with a cat named after an NBA star. Or a family with a phone, debit cards, and a horse and buggy costing as much as a sub-compact car? A family who will answer U.S. Census questions, but still deny a child an education beyond eighth grade?

Was it one or the other? Are they stuck in a make-believe world of old clothes and Biblical truths? Or do they pine to be that Ohio relative of Lena's who hides a cell phone in her purse?

The abiding image I cannot delete of Dan and Lena is of their oats-sowing Rumspringa of the mid 1990s. They drove an aging Cadillac across the Mississippi River heading out for the territory as their ancestors once did from, say, Pennsylvania.

Was the radio blaring grunge, rock or rap music? Could the young couple have concocted a stranger world? Pulling into Los Angeles – Dan and Lena in a Cadillac – harkens an image of Jed Clampett on Beverly Hills Boulevard.

To believe Dan, as they drove the Strip in Las Vegas, they knew they would return to the Amish. Standing in L.A., perhaps at Hollywood and Vine, they knew they would go back to Shipshewana and the flowery intersection of Main and Elm Streets.

Days later, by phone, I asked Dan a question that had bothered me. What would have happened if he, and his then girlfriend, had died on their West Coast Rumspringa? What if they hadn't made it back to Indiana? Back to faith, baptism and marriage? Would they have been destined for heaven or hell?

He thought about it a few days. Eventually he found a disjointed explanation and called. His answer looped endlessly on my cell phone's voicemail: a rambling litany of being Born Again, baptism, service to mankind, God's mercy, and peace on earth. The question had flummoxed him.

To be caught in Las Vegas outside the MGM Grand Hotel in 1996, and be asked by God for an accounting of his life, was not something Dan had thought about.

I forgave him the indiscretion.

"Just because we are Amish, doesn't make us any better than the next person. We are all in this world for the same purpose. For proving grounds, serving our Lord."

****

The memory of the Amish would linger a long time. The next goal was to prove if *Travels with Charley* promoted travel and road tripping in America. One RV expert would tell me that Lucille Ball and Desi Arnaz had already done the job long before Steinbeck went *down John's road.*

●●▶●●●●●●▶●●●●●▶●●●●●▶●●●●●▶●●●●●▶●●●●●▶●●●●●▶●●

10 BIG AL – THE RV PAL

Americans are vagabonds.

Al Hesselbart,
RV/MV Hall of Fame.

****

Americans love Halls of Fame.
Along my route were halls devoted to rock & roll in Cleveland, toys in Rochester, New York and bicycling in Davis, California. Who can forget the Italian-Americans in Sports Hall of Fame in Chicago?

One day, the spacious Recreational Vehicle/Motor Home Hall of Fame drifted by my windshield. Outside Elkhart,

Indiana, the magnificent, 80,000 square-foot Taj Majal sparkled in glass and brick bestride two Interstates.

The RV industry celebrated a centennial in 2010, trying to survive its worst downturn since the 1980s. Back in 1910, the first mass-produced travel trailers were churned out in Los Angeles.

Inside the museum today are dozens of vintage RVs, including a traveling home, paid for by Paramount Studios, for Mae West. It gave mobile meaning to West's *Why don't you come up and see me sometime?*

There is a solid-sided trailer pulled behind a Model T from 1913. Alongside is a futuristic, golden "Star Streak II" RV built on a 1976 Cadillac frame with a huge Oldsmobile engine. At almost three tons deadweight, the builder didn't have gas mileage in mind.

RV raconteur Al Hesselbart, the museum's historian/archivist, granted an interview and tour one morning. We yakked about all things RV.

"Some fifty percent of RV production in the U.S. has an Elkhart home address. It was and is very big here."

Hesselbart said unemployment in the RV industry may have hit thirty percent when the economy nosedived.

My interest resided in truck campers, specifically where Steinbeck's Rocinante and my Gabilan have their roots. Al said the museum has photos and an ad flyer for piggy-back, truck rigs back to 1915.

"I don't believe back in 1915 that they made pickup trucks. It was a runabout with the trunk removed and this contraption sat on it. So the concept of a slide-in truck camper is basically as old as the automobile. The very first campers were quite simply, a box set on top of the bed."

Television cowboy Roy Rogers and wife Dale Evans used to promote truck campers, Hesselbart said.

What about Steinbeck? I asked. Did *Travels with Charley* have effects on the RV industry?

"It surely didn't hurt. But perhaps more than Steinbeck, five years earlier was the Lucille Ball and Desi Arnaz movie, *The Long, Long Trailer*. It took people, not to the bookstores, but to the movie theaters and showed not only low-life trailer trash enjoyed traveling. The working man, the manager, could have fun traveling too."

The 1953 movie *The Long, Long Trailer* was based on a book by Hollywood radio personality Clinton Twiss and his wife Merle. They had bought an Airway Zephyr travel trailer ($4,200) and a new Chrysler New Yorker ($3,500) intending to see the country for two years in the late 1940s. Their travel travails only lasted one year, but the hilarious trek spawned a screenplay.

The movie depicted a sort of *I Love Lucy* on wheels and co-starred Arnaz, Ball and Keenan Wynne, all directed by Vincente Minnelli, Liza's father.

Hesselbart said RVing took off in the late 1950s spurred by baby boomers, easy money, and the expanding Interstate. That was about when Thomas Steinbeck said his father saw a truck and camper on Long Island while contemplating his trip.

Hesselbart said Steinbeck's truck and camper would be similar in form and function to today's rigs.

"There are only so many things you can do with an eight-foot box. The floor plan and functions of a Fifties truck camper are not much different than the plans and functions of a truck camper in 2010."

Steinbeck's other allies were roads and geography.

"We have an opportunity the rest of the world doesn't. We have an amazing highway system. Geographically we have a little bit of everything. If the Germans stay in Germany, they are pretty limited in what they can see. It's hard to go to sunlit beaches in Germany. Most European countries and some Asiatic countries are smaller than some of our states. We have freedom to travel from Maine to California, Washington to Florida. We have enough wilderness and open space that it's not hard, within at least an hour's drive, to find a comfortable place to set up."

John Steinbeck did not consider himself an RVer, a camper, or an American on vacation. He sold Rocinante while the engine was warm, according to Thomas Steinbeck.

It was sold almost immediately. Then as now, you don't really need a vehicle around New York City. I mean, give me break. A pickup and camper in New York City? Not very practical.

Hesselbart said one true thing about Americans, John Steinbeck and me. True as long as campgrounds, credit cards and convenience stores exist.

"Americans are vagabonds."

●●▶●●●●●▶●●●●●▶●●●●●▶●●●●●▶●●●●●▶●●●●●▶●●●●●▶●●

****

Then Al Hesselbart released me to my own vagabond ways. In Pontiac, Michigan I arrived at the GMC factory where my truck first came to life. It was a sad day *down John's road,* relieved only later when a woman gave me a bear hug in the bedroom of America's most ridiculed vice-president.

11   AMBLING THE MIDWEST

Inertia: a property of matter by which it remains
at rest or in uniform in the same straight
line unless acted upon by some external force.

Merriam Webster's
Collegiate Dictionary.

****

My failure was messing with inertia.

Endless Midwest travel cost me time and momentum. I should have taped to my dashboard: *a truck in motion tends to stay in motion.* Instead, for weeks I could have spit into any of the Great Lakes.

Too many commitments had been made. From mid-September to mid-October, I looped and re-looped Wisconsin, Illinois, Indiana, Michigan, and Ohio. Other states beckoned, but I could not respond. Maine and Virginia seemed as remote as Moscow and Venice. Days felt like carnival rides at county fairs; all motion and movement, but no forward progress. Pensive, I wanted Pennsylvania and upstate New York. Instead, I got grain elevators and the drone of distant freight trains deep at night.

Thomas Steinbeck said his father had theories on Americans' love and need for travel. I wondered if it applied to me:

He called it Westering. We discovered the East Coast and then the West Coast. And all that's left is what's inside. Let's go to Nebraska, or Florida. We become like little BBs in a can. The world's biggest game of Pong.

That was me, only worse than BBs in a can or Pong game. I felt like a race car driver; endless laps around a track with no destination. You could sum it up on two license plates' logos. One state I *was* in. The other I wanted to *be* in.

Indiana residents believe in deity: *In God We Trust*.

My mentality was more New Hampshire: *Live Free or Die.*

I was not free and it felt like dying.

****

General Motors was on my mind. The company had announced the closing of its truck assembly plant in Pontiac, Michigan for mid-October 2009. That was significant, because a decal on my driver's door said my truck was built in Pontiac.

John Steinbeck in 1960 wrote about Pontiac and the thriving industrial belt of the upper Midwest:

As I passed through or near the great hives of production – Youngstown, Cleveland, Akron, Toledo, Pontiac, Flint and later South Bend and Gary – my eyes and mind were battered by the fantastic hugeness and energy of production, a complication that resembles chaos and cannot be.

In 2009, the chaos enveloping those cities was an end-game version. The big three automakers teetered on extinction. Ford was better off than GMC and Chrysler, but the future of the Big Three automakers was in jeopardy.

Planning to visit the Pontiac plant on its final day, I headed toward Detroit. Arriving in Oakland County, I found its once proud sports arena – the Pontiac Silverdome – a relic, a sports shadow. The stadium looked orphaned. Its parking lot had grass in the cracks. A huge reader board advertised Saturday flea markets, several steps down from the NFL's Detroit Lions.

Without the address for the GMC Pontiac Assembly Division, I stopped at a branch of a national bank for cash and directions. The tellers had dollars and cents, but zero sense of direction. Five employees proved blissfully unaware of the factory. I might as well have asked for the U.S. Embassy in Algiers, Morocco.

"GMC Assembly Center Pontiac? I'm not familiar with that."

"Is that the one over in ahhh – Whatsanameofdatplace?"

I tried helping.

"My GPS says it might be on Opdyke Road. Does that ring a bell? Look, this place has to be huge. They make thousands of GMC and Chevy trucks there. It must have GMC written everywhere."

"Hey man, I'm just a teller. I don't get involved in that."

One teller was more sheepish than the rest.

"Geez ladies. It's going to be a place so huge and so big, that we are all going to look at each other, and go, duh!"

Those tellers were not going to be bank managers anytime soon. Instead, I drove to the office of *The Oakland Press*. The automobile reporter, Joseph Szczesny, told me the plant would shutter in four days. The next day there would be a picnic for departing employees.

In the morning, I finally found the plant. It went on for city blocks; low-swept, modern, forlorn. Around the factory were busy strip malls and gas stations. Stopping for gas, I asked an attendant a testing question I already knew the answer for.

"When's the GMC plant across the street closing?"

"Heck, I don't know. Are any of them still open?"

"You tell me partner, you're the one who lives here."

"I have a friend who made $100,000 the last two years by not working at GM. What's up with that? What they ought to do is cut salaries of all GM employees in half. The bigwigs and low-lifers. The place would still run fine and they'd have more factories and more jobs to go around."

His version of Economics 101 rolled around my mind as I drove around the giant GMC plant, topped by rows of smokeless stacks. The Receiving Department had nine truck bays. A lone yellow semi-truck filled only one. The other eight were empty. A bereft GMC plant is not on the receiving end of anything.

An immense white tent had been set up. Hundreds of lined-up chairs were mostly empty. The picnic was winding down. Finding real GMC line workers would not be easy, but luck held.

Two middle-aged men, one black, one white, strolled by with paper plates laden with picnic fixings.

"You guys mind chatting?"

"You with the press? We're not supposed to talk with the press. Security is not going to like it if they see your camera."

"Well, I'm not really with the press, but I am a retired journalist driving around the country in this GMC rig writing a book about it."

"Why are you stopping here?"

"I heard the plant was closing. My truck was built here, the door sticker says so. I wanted to shake hands with someone that built my truck and thank them for doing a good job. You guys here back in 2008 when my truck was built?"

"Yes, sir. We were both here."

"A reporter at the newspaper said the plant closes Friday. That true?"

"It closes Friday. But today's the last day a truck is going down the line. They made an announcement a couple of hours ago. They said 'anyone want to have a last look, now was the time.' I didn't bother, I seen too many going down the line."

Kalvin, the black man, was the more outgoing. He would retire the next day after thirty-seven years at General Motors.

"I'm done."

Darra was not so lucky after thirty-three years at GMC. He would transfer to Flint the next week and become a line worker.

"We make a good product," Kalvin said. "Don't listen to anybody else. That last truck going down the line today was just as good as the first one. Believe me."

I asked Kalvin for his emotions after almost four decades at GMC.

"I'm terribly sad. I would have gone on until I wanted to go. We feel like we were forced out. This guy's (Darra) going to Flint not because he wants to go. He's going to keep his job. He's almost like a hobo going down the street."

After thirty-seven years, Kalvin said he had given enough "blood, sweat and tears" for GMC, but still wasn't ready to retire.

"When I hired in at GMC years ago, I was a welder. Before they had the robots, I was the robot. I used to weld by hand. If I was running the company, I would probably have robots too. But you know, there is one thing a robot cannot do and that's buy a vehicle."

Kalvin's passion for GMC and his fellow workers bordered on religious fervor spewed in blue-collar eloquence.

He said GMC was too lop-sided.

"We are top heavy. We have people that don't build anything working in the offices. There are no foot soldiers. It's all chiefs. There are no Indians here."

I had one last question about the auto workers union.

"What about Ron Gettelfinger, the president of the UAW. Isn't he well liked by the rank and file?"

"You mean 'Middlefinger?' We should have a right to vote for who we want to represent us. Just like you have a chance to vote for President. We don't get that chance. They are appointed. We got to dance to the music. It's what I call 'politricks.'"

Why is the distrust of union officials so deep?

"Anytime the union represents you, and you're on strike, and they are still getting paid, then you are not in the same boat. We are losing our houses and everything, but they are going in and negotiating and they are still getting paid."

Darra was not as candid about General Motors at first, but frustration came out as the interview went on. His transfer to Flint was about family economics.

"I would like to work another ten years if my body will take it."

Did he place blame for the company's downturn on executives at GMC's gleaming Renaissance Center in downtown Detroit?

"You know I don't want to talk bad about (GMC CEO Rick) Wagoner. Just a couple of years ago, he said four dollars a gallon gas, that's no problem for Americans. That's the guy running this company. But when it hit four dollars a gallon, I'm not kidding you, within a week truck sales were gone. Who can afford to pay for that new truck, put $200 a week gas in it, and drive it? I don't care what kind of money you are making. It just doesn't float."

Darra said the plant's end had been visible for weeks.

"We saw guys in there with cutting torches already. We heard they are going to gut the place."

Kalvin walked into the mid-afternoon haze, a stack of barbecue ribs dripping sauce off the edge of his paper plate.

"I gave you my phone number. That means if that book sells, I want some royalties."

"He knows all the angles," Darra laughed.

****

I drove north and slept that night at a vintage motel in Gladwin, Michigan – my first motel room of the trip. A year ago, Gladwin was as foreign as Glasgow, Scotland. Now I had visited four times in eight months. Its streets, restaurants and even Chamber of Commerce President, Tom Tucholski, were familiar to me.

More importantly, I had a new friend. Gladwin's former City Manager Howard Smith Sr. was now president of Wolverine Campers. He is a quiet man, usually speaking only when spoken to. He drives an older green Chevrolet truck.

"You know, Steinbeck drove a green truck," I told him.

"Is that right?"

"It's in a museum out in Salinas, California. You ought to

118

go see it. You take a little tour of the museum and the last stop is John Steinbeck's green truck. And sitting on top is that Wolverine Camper your company built. It has a little metal tag on the back, which reads: *Wolverine Campers, Gladwin, Michigan.* I saw it myself."

"You know I ought to get out there sometime and see it myself," Smith said. "I was in California once but never got to Salinas. I didn't have a reason to, but now I do, to see that camper. They called them Pullmans back then. They looked like the Pullman Car on a passenger train."

****

Gabilan maintenance I thought would take days, took four hours. Instantly, I hit the road for Ohio. Leaving Gladwin about an hour before sunset, I decided long ago it was my favorite time. The hours before and after sunset are different. Fields glisten differently, trees stretch higher, shadows languish, and reflections soften. The sun on the roadway reveals every imperfection on the pavement. Hues meld and sounds change. Clamor becomes tranquility. The day is over, its promises met or unfulfilled.

Departing a familiar town is melancholy in the first mile. Less emotional in the second, even less so, the third. On it goes as the town and its people fade into mist. At first, there is yearning to return. The second mile attenuates the first, the third mile softens the second, until, arriving at a point, say ten miles away, one wonders *was I ever really there at all?*

Winding my way through Mount Pleasant and Sturgis,

Michigan on a slow amble to Ohio, rekindled a habit of asking rhetorical questions of every town. Mount Pleasant and Sturgis might be only map dots, but to people born and raised there, a hometown is a lifetime of gravitas.

How many people will die there in 2009? Be born? How many couples divorce? How many residents contemplate suicide?

The questions are endless. How many bookkeepers decide today's the day they begin embezzling? How many young men or women join the Army, or smoke their first joint?

I turn the questions around. How many residents see my rig in the night's gloaming or at dawn, notice my license plate from 2,500 miles away and ponder: *What the heck is that rig doing here?*

****

In a typical Midwest fall, only the hardy insects hang around – chiefly flies. Near Berne, Indiana, I bought two fly swatters, one for the truck, one for the camper. I never saw another fly.

One night, I ate at a Chinese buffet in central Indiana with two young women in an adjacent booth. Both were on cell phones the entire time. Each went to the bathroom multiple times. Eating together, they were never really *together*. The little talking they did was about what each was finding out via cell phone or texting.

I eavesdropped as the two girls talked.

"You ever notice how in Tweeting, you never know how

it's going to go?"

"What do you mean?"

"It takes several lines in before you know if it's negative or positive."

"Oh yah, I get it."

"It's so weird."

"Yah, Tweeting is that way. It's a lot like texting. I just found out this girl at work said her husband is going to leave her because she is ADHD. I watch her at work and believe me, she never gets anything done. She just bounces from task to task. Never finishes anything. Boy, I can relate to her husband."

To me, that was the kettle calling the pot black. This girl, the whole time I watched her, flitted like a bumblebee on steroids. Eating. Texting. Getting more food. Tweeting. Going to the bathroom. Talking about texting. More food. Talking about Tweeting. Kibitzing with a waitress. Going to the bathroom. More cell phone calls.

There might have been two minutes of real conversation about real topics the entire time I listened to these women. What is the point of dining with someone, if you are never *with* them? It's a mystery.

****

Leaving Huntington, Indiana, in my lackadaisical way, I looked for something to pique my interest. It's like being in a library, searching shelves. Turning my head, left then right, tilting this direction and that, I was looking for a *title* about

Huntington. Nothing was promising as I circled the majestic Huntington County Courthouse.

Then a sign flashed by, a foot square at best, with an arrow pointing to the Dan Quayle Museum. The museum was easy to find, but closed. It was Sunday. Next door was the First Presbyterian Church. Two young men were loitering out front.

"Was Dan Quayle born in this town?"

"Yes, but I don't know where."

Inside a woman said Quayle's home "was over on Polk Street somewhere."

Soon enough, I was on Polk Street stopping a young couple smoking cigarettes.

"Did Dan Quayle live on this street?"

"I don't know," the woman said. "You wanna know why I don't know? I don't give a damn. That's why."

Undeterred, I stopped a young mother pushing a stroller. She was equally uninformed.

"I'm from Terre Haute. I don't know anything about this town."

Quayle hunting was proving fruitless when a woman in a car rolled up.

"You the guy looking for Dan Quayle's house? Follow me."

Within minutes we were in front of a tidy, post-World War II postage stamp of a house. A genuine GI Bill/VA loan home if ever one existed.

"That's the Quayle place. It's actually the Keizer's house. I don't know them. But a relative of mine does. Says they are real nice folks. Just go up and knock."

My memory of typical Midwest families is that they go to church Sundays and have a big meal afterward. It was noon. The Keizer's didn't want to be bothered by a stranger.

Still, there were two cars in the driveway. Someone was home. I reasoned that I would never be in Huntington, Indiana again. I knocked.

In perhaps the oddest afternoon of my entire trip, in sixty seconds I was in Dan Quayle's boyhood bedroom being regaled by the effervescent Shirley Keizer. She talked endlessly, energetically and lovingly of Quayle.

"In this very room, Dan once told me, he used to have pillow fights with his brother. Out that window, in that backyard, they played touch football. I heard it got rough once in a while."

Shirley gave me a tour of the home, a history lesson and literally reams of Quayle photos and memorabilia. Shirley was infatuated by Dan Quayle. She and her husband had bought Quayle's boyhood home in 1974.

"I told Dan Quayle once I would never sell this house. I would live and die in this house. We love it here. We are Lutherans and the school is only blocks away. I loved this house from the git go. I told anyone who would listen 'I want that house.' I would not take no for an answer."

Shirley and her more reticent husband Keith believe the home was built in 1945, likely by Quayle's parents. Over the years, Shirley said media from Japan, Germany and *Time* magazine have come by.

"*Playboy* took a photo of my house once," Shirley said

with a touch of Lutheran guilt. One day in the early 1990's, her husband got a call at the dairy where he worked.

"The secret service wants to see you," he was told. "The Quayles want to come back to your house. They wanted to kick off his re-election campaign from here."

There are photos of the Keizers standing with Dan and Marilyn Quayle surrounded by media at 1317 Polk Street. Later they walked around downtown Huntington. They were kicking off the re-election campaign of President George H.W. Bush, with Quayle as his incumbent vice president.

"It was August 23, 1992. I'll always remember that day. The reporters were two or three rows deep. It was sensational."

After one of Quayle's visits, Shirley said he put his hand out to shake hers. She refused and gave a hospitality lesson.

"Mr. Vice-President, I come from a big family and we hug. So I gave him a bear hug. I must say, the Secret Service frowned on that. I didn't care. As far as I'm concerned, he can come back anytime. He'll always get a hug."

I can attest that Shirley Keizer likes to hug. While we were in Quayle's bedroom, at one point Shirley decided I too warranted a Keizer *Special*. She gave me a bear hug of such proportion, warmth, and duration, that I blushed. It was a good thing her granddaughter was in the room with us.

While Quayle was vice president and even later, Shirley noticed limousines driving by that would never stop.

"I always thought it must be him. He was so cute. I would adopt him anywhere, anytime. He was and is the most capable Christian man I know. I'd vote for him to this day."

****

When I left the Dan Quayle Fan Club behind, I left the heartland. John Steinbeck claimed Ohio was the clear dividing line between guarded, standoffish Easterners and friends-in-a-minute Midwesterners. It was time to test that theory in a barber's chair in Conneaut, Ohio – *down John's road.*

●●▶●●●●●▶●●●●●▶●●●●●▶●●●●●▶●●●●●▶●●●●●▶●●●●●▶●●

12   GO EAST YOUNG MAN

Nothing so liberalizes a man and expands the
kindly instincts that nature put in him as travel and
contact with many kinds of people.

Mark Twain, 1867.

****

S
ix weeks into the trip, I finally felt *east*. At worst, I
was in the shadow of the East.

With Lake Erie finally on the left, not Lakes
Michigan or Huron, I was in a portion of America I hadn't
seen for thirty years. It seemed far removed from my
Midwest roots and Pacific Northwest home of two decades. It

was so foreign, if asked, I would have surrendered my passport at the Pennsylvania state line.

As a parting Midwest gesture, in Indiana I uprooted a sprig of soybeans. Weeks later, I twisted off a cotton plant branch near Plainfield, Texas. That flora and a stone I took from Steinbeck's Sag Harbor driveway were all I brought home, except eighty newspapers and 1,000 digital photographs.

Tourist bric-a-brac does nothing for me. Souvenir spoons end up in drawers, imprinted coffee cups in the attic, and T-shirts fray. Real memory lingers in the mind, in a synaptic sinew you can order your life with. Physical proof is not required. My memory's hard drive is not erasable.

****

Moving toward Pennsylvania at last, no appointments awaited, no circled calendar dates could ensnare me. Only Steinbeck's route from my dog-eared *Travels with Charley* and a debit card carried me. More than enough.

Wanting to meet strangers, eat regional food, and listen to accents, I fully realized dawdling might bring New England's fall leaves down before I arrived there.

A rough plan was to park my rig outside Yankee Stadium in late October at about the fifth inning of a World Series game if the Bronx Bombers were playing. A neighbor had dared me to do so. I dreamed of Maine lobster, Baltimore crab cakes and gazing into the dank Manhattan hole that is Ground Zero. In the end, I did none of those things. Planning proved futile. In the end, the trip simply took me.

Before getting to a state, I would think of things tourists normally do. Once I actually arrived, my tourist frame of mind vanished. Rightly so. Tourists no more inhabit, or truly experience a place than a potato does a casserole. Both are just passing through.

****

Geneva-on-the-Lake, Ohio rose off the map, so I headed there. The town proved a ghost. Steinbeck had come across such towns in New England just after his trip began.

Looking around this empty Ohio resort town, only three bars were open. Out on Lake Erie, a single narrow lake freighter fought west against the wind. Two policemen circled in a patrol car. With no people around, crime was hard to imagine.

Placards revealed I had just missed the Thunder on the Strip Bike Rally, featuring *Reckless Rene Regimbal and his World Famous Wall of Death.*

Nearby was Mike's Authentic Gyros. How authentic could a gyro be served by a guy named Mike, fully 8,000 miles from Athens? A palm and tarot card reader promised *Past, Present & the Future. One visit will convince you.*

The town was a scene from Peter Bogdanovich's *The Last Picture Show* with Cloris Leachman and Cybill Shepherd lolling about a dying Texas oil town. Leaving Geneva-on-the-Lake at exactly five fifteen p.m., I passed The Survivors Club tavern.

Outside, the two cops I had seen roving earlier were

arresting a woman. She looked twenty-five and sat on the ground handcuffed and emotionless. The cops stood her up, dipped her head and pushed her into the cruiser's back seat. The Survivor's Club had not lived up to its reputation for that woman.

At the town's edge I met Larry. He was closing for the winter a family amusement center he had owned for thirteen years.

"I was a screw-up in high school. I told my kids you will not be a screw-up. You will go to college and all three did."

He gave me a tour of his pool, his water slide, his go-cart track.

"The go-carts and the merry-go-round, those are my big money makers. My wife and I would really like to put in another eighteen-hole, mini-golf set up. Yes, we would."

"It's all about speed, or at least the perception of speed. I will go to open-wheeled go-carts next season. The old ones are eight years old and are starting to feel the wear and tear. You always have to come up with something new, or perception of new."

It was only mid-October, but the day was frigid. Why so cold, so soon, I asked.

"The lake effect. Oh yes. I've lived around here or close to here all my life. I know all about the lake effect. Most winters we get snow and we get cold. Lots of it. Sometimes not both in the same years. The last true, really harsh winter was back in 1987. Yes sir, 1987 since we had a bad one."

Before he was a small amusement park owner, Larry worked construction in Cleveland.

"Did you work on the new baseball or football stadiums?"

"No, and as far as professional sports are concerned, I'm done. There were two things. First, when the baseball players went on strike in 1994. When those SOBs making all that money had to go on strike, I said I will never pay for another game again. I go if someone will give me a ticket. But pay? Me? Not on your life."

"What was the second thing?"

"It was the nerve of that Terrell Owens (NFL player) saying a few years back, he could not support his family on seven million dollars a year. For crying out loud, I will never make that in a lifetime. Not even close to that. Give me a break Terrell."

****

As I left Ohio, I recalled John Steinbeck pegged the state as a literal and figurative border between East and Midwest. He described New Englanders as not unfriendly or discourteous, just terse. Not true of Ohioans, Steinbeck wrote:

Almost on crossing the Ohio line it seemed to me that people were more open and more outgoing, The waitress in a roadside stand said good morning before I had a chance to, discussed breakfast as though she liked the idea, spoke with enthusiasm about the weather, sometimes even offered some information about herself without my delving. Strangers talked freely to one another without caution.

●●▶●●●●●▶●●●●●▶●●●●●▶●●●●●▶●●●●●▶●●●●●▶●●●●●▶●●

Wanting to test Steinbeck's Ohio theory, my laboratory of choice became a barbershop. In dire need of a haircut anyway, I reasoned a barber's chair was a good place to take a town's pulse.

Not a single barbershop pole spun in Geneva-on-the-Lake, Ohio. Tourists and barbers had scattered. I moved through downtrodden Ashtabula to Conneaut, Ohio just before crossing into Pennsylvania on U.S. 20. On State Street I found The Hair Shack. In minutes I was in the chair under the scissors and combs of Pam, the proprietor.

"Pam, I'm here for one reason. John Steinbeck came through Ohio back in 1960 and said Ohio is the dividing line between friendly Midwesterners and guarded Easterners. In my native Wisconsin, in five minutes you are on a first-name basis with strangers. Is it that way in Conneaut?"

"Most people don't come through trying to prove a theory, but I'll try. I always considered here (Conneaut) and myself as east. But I also consider myself basically friendly. You don't have to earn it with me. The farthest west I've been is Fort Wayne, Indiana. I've done the East Coast thing. Went all the way to the ocean. Been to Massachusetts and New Hampshire. They always seemed too much in a hurry there. In the restaurants and businesses, it was always: 'Are you ready to go? Are you done yet?' I hate that. I couldn't wait to get back to Conneaut, where they give you all the time in the world to do whatever it is you want to do."

I asked Pam how she learned her trade. She traveled to Erie, Pennsylvania to learn cosmetology.

"It was only $1,250 there and they wanted $1,500 around

here. I told myself, I just want to cut men's hair. Keep it simple. I used to do those perms and all that layering stuff. But it wasn't for me. One too many sixteen-year-old girls got into the chair. You know? The ones who you could never please."

Every day, Pam gives about two dozen men's haircuts.

"Are you making a go here in town?"

"I just seemed to time it right. A lot of barbershops were closing up. A few more barbers were ready to retire. It's been good for me. I charge eleven dollars. With all the men out of work, or having a hard time finding work, I have never felt right about raising my prices. I would be cutting my own throat."

I asked Pam about Ashtabula, which seemed the most economically distressed city I had seen in seven weeks on the road.

"It's pretty sad around here right now."

"Is it all connected to the downturn in the auto industry?"

"Oh yes. We were always too tied to the automotive industry. When that went bad, we went bad right with them. We used to do so many plastics around here. A lot of that is gone now. The young people don't stick around. You've got to go where the jobs are. I don't blame them. The older people, a lot come back. They'll go to Florida or Texas and have their career. But when they retire, many come back to Conneaut. They don't have to pay income tax here. That's one of the nice things about Conneaut."

My haircut done, I looked around the tiny shop with its warped floor. Pam sold candles and knick-knacks on the side.

Old *Reader's Digest* magazines and romance novels filled a bookcase.

"You drive safely now," Pam said. "Someday I want to do that. Just travel around. But it won't be in a truck. I'd do it in a car."

"Will this haircut last me until I get home in early December?"

"Nope, I don't think so. You'll have to climb up into another chair somewhere. I would say probably right about Thanksgiving."

Neither the haircut nor my trip lasted that long. I was home in Washington state by November 19. I gave Pam fifteen dollars and an explanation.

"That's eleven dollars for the haircut and four dollars for book research."

****

It had taken forever to get east, but when it arrived, I was east in a hurry. The last miles of Ohio gave way to Pennsylvania. It took two hours to pass through the northwest nub of the Quaker State before arriving in New York. The city of Erie, New York, with blocks of empty factories, matched Ashtabula's bleakness.

Then it was Niagara Falls, which had even less attraction for me than for John Steinbeck. He went there just because he never had before. He stopped. He stared. He moved on.

At the Falls, it bellowed windy and cold amid bright sunshine. A few hardy tourists peered over the edge of the

American or Canadian Falls. Most people had accents. I thought I heard Russian and a couple I talked into taking my photo said they were from Turkey.

Having previously been to Niagara Falls in 1977, I could vouch they were unchanged. The *Lady of the Mist* sailing into the maelstrom under the falls appeared to be the same boat I had ridden years ago.

Though I had gotten a special driver's license to pass into Canada without a passport, I decided to not mimic Steinbeck's aborted trip of 1960. He did not have the proper papers for Charley. It was not a dog or documents stopping me at the border, but bitter cold.

Rolling northeast of Niagara Falls, winter's harbingers arrived. It seemed just days ago I wrestled with flies and ninety degrees in Montana. Now municipal trucks were sporting the metal rigging for snowplows. Private pickups already had plows attached. It was October 14. Signs read *Snowplow Turnaround Areas* or *Snow Tires for Sale – Good Selection.*

In front of hardware and garden stores sat rows of snow blowers where in prior states had been lawnmowers. Flocks of geese landed in cornfields plucking precious kernels before departing south.

Near Mexico, New York, a sign bragged *Voted New York's Most Drinkable Tap Water in 1991 and 1992.* In this Mexico, evidently, you can drink the water.

Up the road in Greece, New York, I salivated for an authentic gyro sandwich and found none.

For one day, I had passed through cities whose industrial

infrastructure and failure to diversify left them in the wake of a new electronic, digital and service-based economy.

The next two nights, I would stay overnight in New York communities whose vibrancy was linked to a new socio-economic model. In both Albion and Malone, New York, I slept near prisons. A growth industry for sure.

****

The miles began to fall away, though not as gently as when the trip began *down John's road.* In Ellsworth, Maine, a friend climbed into the truck cab, only to leave as quickly as he had arrived. He left an essence which sustained me as I drove to the rooftop of the United States.

13   NEW ENGLAND

Like all great travelers, I have seen more than I
remember, and remember more than I have seen.

Benjamin Disraeli,
British Prime Minister.

****

In mid-October, I arrived in New England. Crossing the
bridge at Rouses Point, New York which carries into
Vermont, I drove down narrow strips of land into
Burlington on U.S. 2. Then it was a short trek on I-89, before
bucolic Route 302 into Littleton, New Hampshire.

My logbook of state line crossing shows I spent little time

in Vermont – three hours and 113 miles. I reasoned Maine, where I would gallivant for days because of its sheer mass, could serve as quintessential New England. What I would see there could pass for Vermont and New Hampshire.

Wrong.

What poor logic. One state cannot stand in for the other. Maybe my brain neurons froze as the weather turned ornery. Waking up at a campground near Littleton, my truck's onboard thermometer read twenty-two degrees. For the first and last time, my windshield iced over. The day eventually grew warmer to the liking of the elderly employee at the farmer's co-op where I bought propane.

"Well that sun will do us a world of good today. It feels good," he said.

"I've been on the road from Seattle since September 1. In Montana, it was nearly 100 degrees. Boy, it's quite a swing down to twenty-two."

"Yah, that would be a shock to the system. The news said they were going to try and play baseball today in eight inches of snow. You hear about that? Must have been New York. Could have been Philadelphia too. This is unusual for this time of year. Setting all kinds of records. Nice rig you got there. Traveling alone?"

"Yah. I'm retired from the newspaper business and my wife wasn't feeling well enough to make the trip."

"I used to work in the paper industry in a way. Over in Gilman at the paper factory. Worked there thirty-five years, five years at another place – forty years altogether in paper."

"Did you make newsprint?"

"No, not too much of that. Mostly we made specialty papers. We were making a lot of check paper. You know, for government checks with the fancy backgrounds. That has to be special, all kinds of safeguards. There's a lot of safety stuff that goes into that paper that the public never knows about."

I mentioned I had once visited the U.S. Mint in Washington, D.C. watching millions of dollars rolling off presses, armed guards strolling behind thick glass.

"Funny you mentioned that, because we started making paper for money right here in Gilman. Real paper for real money. Shipped that stuff straight to Washington, D.C. That made security and safety at the factory go way up."

"You worked forty years in the industry. You must have been foreman when you quit."

"I did make foreman for a time. But I went back to working in the yard, because I liked that shift better. At one point I was making twenty bucks an hour. You don't find that kind of pay anywhere anymore. No sir. Eventually we got bought out by Simpson Paper Company. Aren't they out there in Seattle someplace by you?"

"I see their trucks now and then."

"We made a good product. Not anymore. You know all those decisions and the decision-makers upstairs. You know what they do. They bought a plant down in Texas, tried to get that place going. They spent millions and millions. Never got it right. Well, I got to get back to work. You have a safe trip now."

I drove to Gilman to see the factory where he worked. The

138

parking lot was empty, the windows of the factory shot out. Gates had heavy, rusted padlocks.

Nearby, I stopped to get gas at a one-pump station and hung around talking to the manager. His business had been up and down in recent years as the paper factory struggled.

"What I worry about is the kids coming up today. They go to school for twelve years, get a good education and what are you going to do for them when the work goes overseas? This is the worst part. The products they make overseas might be better than ours. That's saddest of all."

I took too much time talking to the store manager. A line had formed outside behind the one-pump island. A bearded man, first in line, was not happy.

"You sure took your diddle-dawdle time about it. It didn't do me any good to hurry over here. Move it will yah?" His words were the angriest I heard on my entire trip.

Engaging him in conversation proved pointless. He refused, slammed his door and rolled up his window. He was a taciturn New Englander, one of few I met. His ill temperament was cancelled out by a man I met later that day when parked at the Catholic Saint Anthony's Soup Kitchen in Skowhegan, Maine. He was riding bicycles with his young children.

"Need directions?"

"No, I've got a GPS. Thanks for asking."

"Suit yourself."

A day later, another couple pulled over when they saw me huddled over the atlas.

"Where you headed?"

"I don't know."

"I see you're from Washington state. Maybe we can lead you to where you gotta go."

"That would be nice. But I don't know where I gotta go. I haven't figured it out yet, but I appreciate you asking."

"Suit yourself."

There it was again "suit yourself." Seemed to be the libertarian phrase of the month in New England.

****

Driving all day, I arrived in Ellsworth, Maine on a Saturday night. I chose a Protestant church to attend in the morning. A surreal moment waited.

Arriving early at church, I spied two middle-aged men in an older car. They scoped me out just as I sized them up. They both walked into church and I followed them in.

After church only one man, the older of the two, returned. What happened to the other man? My mind flared in a new direction. For unfathomable reasons, that missing man became John Steinbeck to me.

Leaving the church parking lot, I convinced myself Steinbeck was the missing man and he was sitting beside me. The ease with which I could carry on a conversation with him felt eerie.

I was nearing the mid-point of my journey and I was slipping into emotional limbo. Traveling Steinbeck's route, talking to people, hearing stories from the American Road, I had total freedom to travel any distance at any speed. In

Ellsworth, I felt more like a prisoner. Loneliness had set in. Though I was free to sleep in Gabilan, stay at a hotel, or visit friends and relatives, at times, I did not feel free.

That Sunday, I needed someone to talk to. Needed my wife, a friend, someone who knew me. Or, I needed Steinbeck's Charley – perhaps my unruly Black Labrador Retriever Zorro. Instead, what did I have? The yawning open road and an empty passenger seat. Out of perceived need, I concocted a companion.

As I left church on that cool, brisk, mid-October Sunday, I was fifty-seven years old and whining. Two days before, my wife had declared herself "off the radar screen." She didn't want to hear from me by phone or e-mail. I didn't blame her. I can be wimpy at times. The calendar and atlas said I was weeks from home. I was losing my grip. On what, I did not know exactly.

On my trip thus far, I found myself praying a lot, often minute-by-minute for my family, for this project to make sense, for the towns I drove through and the people I saw and met.

On this Sunday, the pastor ended his sermon by saying, "Go out in the world and become fishers of men." The pastor said only two percent of professing Christians have influenced another person to Christianity.

I was in Ellsworth, Maine, thousands of miles and $50,000 into my *Travels with Charley* project. Anxiety often felt like iron bands on my chest and hands around my throat, at times leaving me breathless thinking about miles and days yet to endure.

And as I left the church parking lot, on my way to Deer Isle, Maine, it seemed Steinbeck had gotten in the front seat. I created an apparition. Surrounded by one point three million Maine residents, I was an island that needed to find another island, inhabited by at least one person. Enter, John Steinbeck.

It seems far-fetched now, but then I desperately needed a person to talk with. For the first and only time, I began a conversation with John Steinbeck.

"Well, there you are after all, Mr. Steinbeck. I guess we are going to be traveling together for awhile. Welcome aboard."

"But I've done this before. I don't know what's going to be in it for me."

"Well, you said in your book that you went to church every Sunday, but you only talked about one Sunday service in Vermont. Why didn't you provide details of the other services?"

"My publisher would never have gone for that. You can only put so much religion into any book. People don't want to be preached at."

"Are you a Christian, Mr. Steinbeck?"

"I suppose I am. I enjoy the trappings of church. Just don't make me feel guilty."

"But you are guilty. We are all guilty of something."

"You can save that buster, or I'm getting out right now."

"No, don't get out. Please don't get out."

"Am I going to have to listen to this for 4,000 miles?"

"Hey, it's a message I have been hearing in my mind for

years. There is never any way of getting away from the guilt. The guilt of all the things you have ever done wrong."

"I'm not sure I'm the one you can use to unload your guilt."

"Well, Mr. Steinbeck, I can tell you the guilt is killing me. I have to talk to someone about it. And it appears we are stuck together."

Twice before on my trip I had attempted to talk about Christianity to people. Both attempts were halting, awkward, sophomoric in nature. At least I had tried.

I told my best friend in Granville, Ohio how hard it was to reveal to people that you are a Christian. I thought the topic would appeal to him, because he is a devout Catholic. Time cut the conversation short.

Then I had told my camper manufacturer, Howard Smith Sr., when I left Gladwin, Michigan for the last time, that I always prayed for towns as I passed through. I prayed for teachers, pastors, policemen, children, doctors, anybody in town I could think of. He looked at me almost apologetically, and said I was "doing the right thing."

Now I was in Maine, talking to a truck seat, convinced sitting beside me was an American literary icon. He was a Pulitzer prize-winner, Nobel laureate, a man whose books still sell thousands of copies yearly. A man who dipped his books in Christian allegory and metaphor.

I tried sincerely, but couldn't sustain the imaginary conversation with Steinbeck. It waned as I drove about negotiating Maine's coast. I vowed to never set anything on the front passenger seat. For awhile anyway, it was declared John Steinbeck's seat.

****

Eventually, I figured out the route to Deer Isle, Maine which had had a Svengali hold on Steinbeck. I had to go see why Deer Isle left this man of letters struggling for descriptive words. Deer Isle stayed with Steinbeck long after he left. He claimed images about the place often returned to his memory; ones he hadn't remembered being imprinted in the first place.

As I arrived on Deer Isle, its chief harbor, Stonington, was under storm warning. The wind blew whitecaps in the distant inlets. I decided to find a hotel room, hopefully overlooking the harbor. I was ready for a night outside Gabilan, where I had slept nightly since Ohio.

Stonington appeared to be a major player in the lobster fishing world. Scores of lobster boats bobbed at anchor. Around the harbor, knuckle-like rock formations reached out to the sea. Even an experienced, sharp-eyed lobsterman must find them difficult to navigate.

All the restaurants in town were closed on the stormy Sunday evening. Two small hotels remained open. Only one gave me the view of Stonington's harbor I desired. I paid ninety-five dollars for a superb waterside room. It would be my last hotel room for twenty-nine days. The storm settled in deeper. The wind blew harder. Rain began to pelt.

In 1960, Steinbeck stopped a state patrolman for directions

to Deer Isle and found him aloof, standoffish – a nominee for Mount Rushmore, he wrote.

With my hotel room settled, parking my oversized rig on tight Stonington streets presented problems. So I too approached a policeman sitting in his cruiser near the docks. He was anything but aloof.

"Can you recommend a place to park this rig overnight?"

"Just park in any parking spot downtown, we won't bother you."

"But my rig is pretty long, it sticks out."

"Those spots are big enough. Yours doesn't stick out as far as the rigs I see all summer."

"What about this parking lot right here? Can I park here?"

"No way. Not allowed. The lobstermen will be here first thing in the morning. They won't be happy seeing you here. All these spots are reserved. Better to take one of those spots downtown. You'll be fine. Enjoy your stay. Have a good time."

****

About eight p.m. the storm won out over the power grid. Electricity went out for the night. Amenities my ninety-five dollars paid for were kaput. No computer. No television. I needed a flashlight to use the bathroom. There was only my wind-up dynamo radio giving NFL scores. I turned it off.

Opening the curtains, I gazed over the now-dark harbor where a few lobster boats had running lights on. The storm abated eventually, but power did not return until morning.

At breakfast, the proprietress was sorry, but would not reduce my bill. She was a pleasant, regal woman recently elected president of the Chamber of Commerce.

She was fully aware Steinbeck had stopped in Stonington fifty years ago. In fact, she knew the house where he had stayed. She once arranged a meeting with the woman owner to find marketable value in Steinbeck's 1960 visit. It did not go well with the woman.

"Don't tell anyone to come up my driveway. I don't want that."

****

After breakfast, I walked Stonington's rainy docks looking for a lobsterman. A snappy-looking boat named *Reliance* nestled pier side. Aboard was Randy Shepard of Sunset, Maine. He'd been lobstering for twenty years aboard a boat that was twenty years old when he bought it.

I asked how the lobster had been running.

"It was a good summer. Real good catch. But I didn't make any more money than any other year. It all averages out. Last year, the catch was not quite as good, but the prices were up. So it all levels out over time."

"I don't see anybody else aboard. Do you fish alone?"

"Oh no. I used to do that as a kid in a skiff, but I'm a little smarter now. I always take somebody. Sometimes two guys. It only takes one mistake out there on the water. A slip, a fall, a blackout. Who knows? There's always something out there waiting for you."

His years on the water made him fear it even more.

"I myself have fallen off that ladder several times, sometimes tied up to the pier. You fall off that ladder out there, well, I've fished several of my crewmen out of the water over the years. It's impossible to get back into this boat. It has those high sides."

"Why aren't you out fishing today?"

"Can't fish on Sundays. It's bad luck. There's a saying. 'Break it on Sunday, fix it on Monday.'"

He said Maine state laws and tradition dictate no fishing on Sundays from Memorial Day to Labor Day.

"The best fishing is in the summer. In the winter you have to go farther out and it gets nastier and nastier the farther out you go. The NOAA people have buoys out there. They tell you what you need to know."

"The lady at the hotel where I stayed last night said this port loses one guy, per summer, out on the boats. She said they get a foot caught in a line, or have a heart attack. Is it true someone died recently?"

"Oh yes. I knew the guy. We used to sell our catch to the same dock. He wasn't a close friend, but I knew him. They found him, at least the divers did. He was on the bottom. They had a good idea where he was. They found his boat. He was in his forties."

"In winter, you only go out on the good days. Today would not be a good day. It takes such a little thing. Your motor quits, you run aground. A good wind comes up and gets you turned around. In the winter, you have to go out twenty to thirty miles to get into cold water. It's not fun."

"Does lobster fishing run in your family?"

"My father has been a fisherman his whole life. Lobsters, scallops, gill netting. He's done it all."

"Would you want your son to become a lobsterman?"

"I hope to God not. He needs to get a good education. Cure cancer. Anything, but fishing."

****

That day, I drove to the rim rooftop of Maine. Driving Highway 1 seemed up, up, and more up – like climbing Mount Everest in a car. Signs broke the boredom.

Site of the Largest Whirlpool in the Western Hemisphere. Another sign near Saint Croix crowed about *The Most Eastern Golf Course in the Continental United States.*

Easternmost maybe, but don't hit your tee shot into that whirlpool.

Arriving at Presque Isle, Maine for the night, checking the atlas, I labeled the next day "turnaround day." It would be the point I was farthest from home.

I was deep in Aroostook territory. The land seemed elevated, making visibility unending in any direction. I saw empty potato fields mile after mile. When Steinbeck passed through this part of Maine, he was looking for French-Canadian potato pickers.

Handpicking of potatoes in fall 2009? Not a chance. Twice I saw a mechanical potato picker in the field, but no Cajuns.

Rarely is the halfway point of a trip so clearly demarcated. At exactly noon on turnaround day, my truck compass turned from north to south as I angled down Highway 11 in Madawaska, Maine. My odometer read exactly 7,250 miles since departure.

****

In Maine, I learned of a love affair. I read moose news, witnessed moose events, felt moose innuendo everywhere, but never saw a moose. However, I did see:

- Scores of "Moose Crossing" signs.
- A man selling moose antlers near Ellsworth.
- The "Moosifiers," – Department of Wildlife men driving around in dirty Ford trucks.
- Budweiser signs blazing "Welcome Moose Hunters."
- Moose meat processing advertised for fifty-five cents a pound.
- A moose processing truck near Ashland, with pallets of moose entrails nearby.
- Moose scat on the roads.
- A moose taxidermist.
- Several moose-tagging stations.
- A moose statue near Houlton, Maine.
- People afraid of getting shot, mistaken for a moose, out retrieving mail in fluorescent orange garb walking dogs with orange caps over canine ears.

Just when I gave up hope of seeing an actual moose, at dusk, 5:10 p.m., October 20, 2009, something moved in a clearing. My location was latitude 45.398179 and longitude -

●●▶●●●●●▶●●●●●▶●●●●●▶●●●●●▶●●●●●▶●●●●●▶●●●●●▶●●

69.062419 according to my GPS. To this day, I could find it in my sleep.

Was it a bear? A horse? Bigfoot/Sasquatsch out walking? The nearer I drove, full reality hit me. Looming was a huge, molasses, 100 percent ugly – moose! He stared imperiously. My camera might have been a rifle, yet he was fearless of being shot. I focused and snapped his mugshot, drawing ever closer. He stared at me, then dropped his massive head to nibble on the field stubble. He was the brave son-of-a-gun I named *Brownie*.

****

Knowing every mile would bring me closer to home alleviated the loneliness that so ruefully hit me days before.

Even my notion disappeared completely that John Steinbeck had climbed into the vehicle with me. I began to put things in the front seat again; atlas, computer, and logbook Thomas Steinbeck recommended I keep. It was all there, but not John Steinbeck.

I am largely too pragmatic to believe in ghosts or spirits, making it more puzzling to realize how I had conjured up Steinbeck. The mind plays tricks when you are lonesome. Somehow, I believed imagining Steinbeck beside me would ease the melancholy. It would not be so. As I headed back across the United States, I never again felt Steinbeck's aura in the truck. The need had elapsed. Steinbeck lived in my mind and heart deeply enough. He no longer needed to ride psychological shotgun *down John's road.*

●●▶●●●●●●▶●●●●●▶●●●●●▶●●●●●▶●●●●●▶●●●●●▶●●●●●▶●●

****

My midnight misadventures at Walmarts continued in Groton, Connecticut. Handsome, homeless and likely schizophrenic, Dave pushed himself into my trip in a way impossible to forget.

14   SAG HARBOR SEGUE

He loved Sag Harbor. He loved the people of
Sag Harbor. In turn, the people of Sag
Harbor loved and protected him. When
people would ask where he was or lived, we'd
all say, 'Oh sure, we know where he lives.'
Then we'd send them over the bridge the
wrong way.

Artie Moore, Steinbeck
friend in Sag Harbor.

****

B y the map, my trip was half over.

I had driven the northern rim of America, with a long foray into the Midwest and then up the edge of the Great Lakes to Maine. It had taken seven weeks and almost 8,000 miles to arrive at midpoint. Little did I know it would only take thirty days to get home. The longer I was away from home, the faster the pace of my trip. It had to be. It was a survival tool.

Lonely for human company, I found myself kibitzing with anyone and everyone on certain days. I would wander into Walmarts late at night to buy bogus items so I could talk to greeters or cashiers. With no chance of my wife ever joining me on my trip, and half a continent to go, I soldiered on. It was the American way. Be tough. Get a grip.

****

Anxious to get overdue truck maintenance done, I pulled into a tire store in Augusta, Maine. Men went to work rotating my tires and I set off on a four-mile walk to the picturesque State Capitol.

Walking across curving Memorial Bridge over the Kennebec River, the dome of the State Capitol rose above autumn leaves. The setting was jarred when an older car filled with teens rattled by and a youngster leaned out to yell "fag." I figured they were blowing off testosterone on a noontime jaunt. A bit nonplussed, I hadn't been called that term since high school, I walked on.

The Capitol building was of Maine granite and finished in

●●▶●●●●●▶●●●●●▶●●●●●▶●●●●●▶●●●●●▶●●●●●▶●●

1832 for the princely sum of $145,000. The female figure "Wisdom" sits atop the dome clad in copper, plated with gold.

The colors growing more vivid and the prospect of Gabilan again being road-ready quickened my pace. Soon I was on the same graceful Kennebec River Bridge.

My saunter is not really a saunter at all. I have the gait of a fifty-seven-year-old, bow-legged man. My stride, while not grandfatherly, befits the style of a benign great-uncle.

Wearing sneakers, relaxed fit jeans disguising my forty pounds-overweight waistline, thin windbreaker and weathered GMC ball cap, I felt like actor Wilford Brimley. I was aging, but not yet old, with walrus mustache, and jowly cheeks.

As I passed over the bridge in the opposite direction, fully ninety minutes after my first crossing, the same car filled with teens drove by.

"You're still a fag," cried the same young man. I'll have to watch more closely the roles Wilford Brimley has been playing lately.

I passed through Biddeford, Maine and drove down the rest of the Maine coast, into New Hampshire on my way to Brattleboro, Vermont. Making good time, I forged on to Deerfield, Massachusetts to see Eaglebrooke School where John Steinbeck's son John IV had attended. It was one of Steinbeck's first stops on his journey fifty years before.

Like Steinbeck, I arrived late in the day. Not many people were around, although several cars had parents offloading or reloading sons.

Offices were closed so I camped nearby and returned to the school the next day. You get to Eaglebrooke by driving up a tight, winding road with a small tunnel through an overhead concrete train trestle to negotiate. I parked outside the admissions office.

Turns out it had been parents' weekend and many of the people I might have talked to weren't there. So, I was given an admissions brochure, took a few photos and was on my way to New London, Connecticut to catch a trio of ferries to Sag Harbor, Long Island, New York, and a much-anticipated destination.

Rolling into Groton, Connecticut late in the evening, I pulled into a Walmart. One of my trip's most haunting moments ensued.

In the distance, a man pushed a shopping cart on a straight line toward me. The day had been long, the evening was over and I had three ferries to take in the morning. The man was talking to himself, whistling and singing. I didn't want to be hassled for change, or smell the reek of alcohol as he told a forlorn story. But he rolled straight at me as I leveled up my rig for the night.

He was black, handsome, young, and engaging. His name was Dave. I liked him from the first minute and that minute was near midnight.

"Where can you get a rig like this?"

"Michigan."

"So that's where they come from?"

"Well, they come from all over, but this one was built in Gladwin, Michigan."

"You had this built special didn't you?"

"How did you know my camper was custom-built?"

"Because it is so nice. I always wanted one of these. I had an uncle that had one once, but he never gave me ride. Can you rent one?"

"Well, I suppose you could, but then you'd have to rent a truck to go along with it."

"They come separate?"

"I should say so. How much you think this cost me?"

"$100,000?"

"Well about half that."

I gave him a quick tour.

"I'll bet you can really get the women on the open road in this thing."

"I'm happily married. There is no need for that."

After I asked him where he lived, the story unwound about why the winsome young man was pushing a shopping cart through a midnight Walmart.

"Well temporarily I am living over in New London. It just hasn't been working out in some of the other places."

"Where are the other places?"

"Anywhere I can find."

"Are you homeless?"

"Not really. I always manage to find someplace to sleep."

"Are there homeless shelters in New London?"

"Yes and no. Sometimes they let you in. Sometimes they don't. Sometimes they're full. Sometimes they ain't."

"How are you going to get to New London?"

"Bus Eleven and then transfer. I haven't figured out the

other bus number yet. It might take two, three hours."

I thought about giving him a ride, or letting him sleep overnight with me. Both ideas were never uttered aloud.

"You have relatives nearby?"

"Well that's another one of those questions you can answer yes or no."

"You got a job?"

"Every now and then I'll work, but it won't be just any job. Maybe I'll put in an application here. I only been to this Walmart once. The last time I was here, I got into a truck with a couple guys. Then I got out and they took off with all my stuff. It wasn't much. But it was all I had. I never saw them again."

"Did you ever think about joining the military? The Army or the Navy?"

"Yes, I think about it. Thought about it a lot. But sometimes they tell me my thinking isn't quite right. What about you? Why are you in Groton?"

After revealing my reason and showing my route, I pointed out the small Puget Sound seaport where I live and asked, "You ever been out to Seattle?"

"No. Once I was in San Fran. It was OK, but I didn't think it was everything everyone told me it was going to be."

His ball cap gave away his fandom.

"You a Yankee fan?"

"Oh yah. I grew up on Long Island. You gotta be a New York fan one way or another. I think the Yankees got it this year."

"But that guy Swisher popped out last night with the bases

loaded in the top of the ninth."

"Yah. Tell me about it, I watched it on TV."

"Where?"

"Same place I always do. Anyplace I can find with a TV."

We mused for a few moments about the approach of winter.

"How do you stay warm in that rig?"

"Gas. Propane gas."

"One night I was staying at a shelter, and these guys were ragging on me. So I poked my nose out the door. I was going to the streets. But my nose froze and my toes froze just like that. So I went back inside and put up with them. Some things you just gotta do. Like you. You're taking a journey about John Steinmen."

"No, Steinbeck. You know, he wrote *The Grapes of Wrath, East of Eden, Of Mice and Men.*"

"I gotta admit, I never heard of them. And I like to read man, I really do. I'll have to look him up at the library. That's another place to stay warm. Staying warm, that's the thing. Some of us are. Some aren't. You ever notice this country is screwed up. It's that whole injustice thing. There is justice for some people. There is justice for other people. Problem is there is not justice for all people all the time. It's simple. There should be justice for everyone."

"Well, we got Barack Obama in there now. He's all about justice."

But Dave was skeptical.

"We'll see, man. We'll see."

The night grew darker and cooler. His rendezvous with

Bus Eleven approached. Killing time, we riffed on Kareem Abdul-Jabbar, Mike Tyson, and Alex Rodriguez. We rambled about sports millionaires while he hunkered over his half-full shopping cart. He was truly a handsome young man with an open, round face and matching smile and personality.

"Anyone ever tell you look like a young Muhammad Ali?"

"Yah, lots of people. Other people tell me I look like Babe Ruth. You ever hear of Babe Ruth?"

"What do you mean, did I ever hear of Babe Ruth? Do I look like I was born behind a barn, or on the moon? That's like asking did you ever hear of God."

"Well, you look at Ali and Babe Ruth. They look the same. People tell me and I look like both of them."

"Maybe you ought to start calling yourself Babe Ali," I quipped.

"Or Muhammad Ruth?" he jabbed back laughing.

I tried to stump him on sports trivia.

"Who is the second-leading scorer in the NBA of all time?"

"That guy Magic who got the HIV?"

"No. He quit too soon."

"Oh yah, it must have been, Michael Jordan."

"No, he retired in his prime. Plus he quit to play baseball for a couple of years."

His bus careened into the parking lot and circled. Abruptly, he took off pushing his cart ahead.

"The second leading scorer is Karl Malone," I yelled.

"Oh yah, The Mailman."

Dave was disappearing forever, but managed to sneek in a

last trivia question.

"Who was number three?" he asked, his voice fading in the midnight mist.

"I don't know."

"I think it was Jerry West."

It seemed unreal. A young man yelling about Jerry West over the din of the midnight bus in Groton, Connecticut. He disappeared around the rear bumper of the bus, his shopping cart left in the grass. I went over to see if he had left a remnant of identity. The cart was empty. So were the night and my soul.

I had known Dave for eight or ten minutes, and surely, I will never see him again. Yet, with God as my witness, he haunts me. Dave. Homeless, possibly schizophrenic Dave. Screaming about Jerry West as Bus Eleven rolled into the night. Would Dave ever think of me again? Life does not permit such answers. It only gives these. Michael Jordan is number three in NBA scoring; Jerry West is fifteen.

****

The day arrived for the spiritual epicenter of my journey. I was destined for Sag Harbor on Long Island, New York.

From a modest home on Bluff Point, Steinbeck began his journey September 23, 1960. Steinbeck sighed as his wife Elaine jauntily drove away to New York City. Steinbeck knew he was going the other direction.

●●◗●●●●●●◗●●●●●◗●●●●●◗●●●●●◗●●●●●◗●●●●●◗●●●●●◗●●

ABOVE: John Olson takes delivery of a Wolverine Camper. Left, Howard Smith Jr. Right, his father, Howard Smith Sr. BELOW: Smith Sr. standing outside the building which housed Wolverine Campers in the late 1950s. Steinbeck's camper Rocinante was likely built inside.

ABOVE: The Schwartz family of Shipshewana, Indiana. Back row: Lindsey, Dan, Lena and Dallas. Front row: Jenny and Titus. BELOW: John Steinbeck's Sag Harbor, Long Island home, where, in October 2009, John Olson hung his GMC ball cap on the tree at left.

In October 2009, college student John Carr takes a smoke break on The Appalachian Trail near Front Royal, Virginia. Carr had been walking alone since June, starting in Maine, on his way to Georgia eating macaroni and cheese and reading existentialist books.

New Orleans cabdriver Robert M. outside William Frantz Public School on November 6, 2009. At the school, John Steinbeck witnessed racism in 1960. Numbers on building indicate it was checked for bodies after Hurricane Katrina by Fort Worth, Texas firefighters.

ABOVE: Gary, a long-haul trucker in Winslow, Arizona. Inside his rig were 40,000 pounds of chicken bones headed for a dog food factory in Arkansas. BELOW: Outside Arcata, California, Olson ponders his 80-day journey: 34 states, 12,673 miles and one quart of oil burned.

John Olson sits inside John Steinbeck's camper Rocinante at the National Steinbeck Center in Salinas, California. The typewriter is a bit of ruse. It was not aboard during Steinbeck's 1960 trip. For most of his life, John Steinbeck wrote his significant literature in longhand.

Waking in Groton with no sign of Dave, I drove straight to the New London Cross Sound Ferry Terminal. First there would be a long ferry ride to Orient Point and then two smaller, shorter ferries to Sag Harbor.

I pulled up to a huge waiting lot. An attendant greeted me.

"I'll have to measure you."

"I can tell you I am exactly twenty-two feet long."

"Well you look honest enough. I'll take your word for it. Get in Lane Eight and I'll call it in to the office. Go inside for your ticket."

Inside, the woman at the desk quoted me an astounding price of seventy dollars.

"I'm only twenty-two feet. What do semi-trucks pay?"

Our conversation was cut off by the parking lot attendant calling in on his radio.

"Hey there's a guy coming in with a black pickup and camper. He says it's twenty-two feet long. I didn't measure it. I believed him. He is about fifty-five or so, kind of handsome."

My face flushed. Handsome? Me? The Wilford Brimley look-alike? The fag. I blushed to the lady behind the counter, muttering something about the guy must be talking about someone else.

"Well, you snowed him. He usually measures everyone."

"Well, you tell him, he's handsome too. But in a manly kind of way."

"Men!" she cackled, shaking her head.

On the boat, the hulking *John H*, I never sat down once for the ninety-minute crossing. On this passage, fifty years ago,

Steinbeck had found a sailor to talk to. I was still trying to close that loop. Groton was still a Navy town. I had seen the bases the night before. Surely a sailor, maybe two were aboard. There were none.

I asked several young men with short hair, but got blank stares and rambling answers.

"No. Not in the Navy. But my two buddies inside tried to join the Army once, does that count?"

Another man had a jacket on with Coast Guard insignia.

"Still a Coastie?" I asked.

"No, I'm out now. I used to serve up in Gloucester and Falmouth. But I'm done with that. I still work at a marina. I'm still on the water. Not in the Navy, but will that work for you?"

Nope that won't work.

Another young man with short hair turned out to be a marine engineer at General Dynamics Electric Boat – the nuclear submarine builder in Groton.

"Sorry I can't help you."

As we passed by the shipyard where he was employed, I couldn't see a single submarine.

"Where are all the subs?"

"Oh, they're there. You don't see them. But they're there. I get a paycheck every week to prove it."

****

Departing the *John H* at Orient Point, after two quick ferry rides, a traffic circle, a bridge and quickening heart rate, I was in Sag Harbor. The leafy community sniffed of glitterati with BMW and Lexus proving the people's car.

It seemed a village where people drink tea and wine with pinkie extended. I usually hate those kinds of towns – I made an exception for Sag Harbor.

In this town Steinbeck got hounded for autographs. Once he signed as Ernest Hemingway and joked the recipient hardly noticed. Once he complained "I'm getting sick of my own name."

Trying to find a spot to park my rig would not be easy. One parking lot, still flooded from recent rains, had a sign banning parking from midnight to four a.m. I found a cop. He was no help; in fact, he said I would get a ticket.

The venerable John Jermain Memorial Library was a gem. On the second floor a John Steinbeck bust sat on a pedestal. The library did have a surprisingly small vertical file on Steinbeck. A librarian sent me in the general direction of John Steinbeck's house. I drove there in the pelting rain, but decided to wait until the next day to take a photo.

The next day, Sunday, I went to church and then for a long walk along a beach. I met a couple who told me about all the famous people who have lived or visited over the years: Alan Alda, Christie Brinkley, Billy Joel, and Roy Scheider (the police chief in *Jaws*).

Other people said Colin Powell, Robin Leach, and Paul Simon had been spotted about town.

As I drove back into Sag Harbor to find a place to park for the night, I stopped near a picturesque bridge to capture a photo of the sun's fade to the west.

Talking with a pair of tow truck drivers in a convenience store parking lot, I glimpsed a familiar face. Out of a Jeep popped one of America's most famous journalists, Carl Bernstein. He was on his way into the 7-11 store to get the Sunday *New York Times*.

Turns out one of the tow truck drivers knew him, so when Bernstein returned, he introduced us. We took a photo and that was that.

Ten minutes later, I stopped at the only hamburger joint in town open that night – a place called Bay Burger.

There was Bernstein again.

"You following me?" he asked.

"You following me?" I returned.

He invited me to sit down and for ten minutes we talked about Steinbeck, writing books, journalism, what to do between here and New Orleans and general topics. He gave me his personal e-mail address and we parted.

Bernstein seemed interested in my journey. He talked about a similar trip across Canada when he was a young man.

"Writing a book is hard. It doesn't come easy. The key is getting a good editor. Making the jump from journalism to writing books is difficult. But eventually you develop a rhythm."

When I told of my anxiety about the Deep South, he offered assurance.

"Do it, you'll be fine. Go to New Orleans and eat, eat, eat."

He had one recommendation for the long trek from Long Island to New Orleans.

"Take the Skyline Drive or the Blue Ridge Parkway. You won't regret it."

****

My last day in Sag Harbor I had a plan. I would visit the venerable *Sag Harbor Express* and check their archives for what was happening September 23, 1960 – the day Steinbeck blew town. Then I would return to his Bluff Point home for a photo.

The day turned out differently. I did go the newspaper and met the editor, a reporter and sportswriter Benito Vila. Benito was also a Steinbeck fan.

"Steinbeck discovered the Sixties before the Sixties even happened," he said.

Late in the afternoon, I was outside a barber shop reading a *New York Times* article about Steinbeck posted in the window.

"Something I can help you with?"

"I'm just interested in this article about John Steinbeck. I'm in town studying him a little bit."

"Well, I can help you. I served on the Whaling Festival committee with Steinbeck. I knew him well. Knew his wife Elaine well too. Steinbeck used to call me 'The Alien' because every January I had to go register at the Post Office. I was a Canadian."

Artie Moore, age sixty-eight, proved a winsome companion for several hours. He was a retired tool and die maker and he knew plenty about Steinbeck. Moore had

171

moved to Sag Harbor from Montreal and became acquainted with Steinbeck early on.

"He loved Sag Harbor. He loved the people of Sag Harbor. In turn, the people of Sag Harbor loved and protected him. When people would ask where he was or lived, we'd all say, 'Oh sure, we know where he lives.' Then we'd send them over the bridge the wrong way."

Moore said Steinbeck's favorite bar was The Black Buoy, a few paces away from where we stood. Moore laughed, when I said I'd been doing research at *The Sag Harbor Express*.

"We locals used to call the paper *The Sag Harbor Distress* because there were so many typos and grammar problems. It was proofread all right. Ninety proof."

Moore and I walked down to a windmill at the end of the main street where a plaque dedicated to Steinbeck notes his Whaling Festival contributions.

As I left town, I went to the Steinbeck property on Bluff Point one last time. Birds chirped. A deer statue ornamented the lawn. A few leaves nestled on the roof.

This time, I ventured forth on the property, boldly trespassing. I took photos and grabbed a stone from the driveway. Something real. Later I inscribed it:

10.26.09

Bluff Point

"Sag"

It sat over my desk the entire time I wrote this book.

****

Leaving Sag Harbor, Long Island behind, The Big Apple beckoned. My camera was loaded for Yankee Stadium. But New York City chewed me up and then spit me out like a watermelon seed into the fields and streams of New Jersey and Pennsylvania *down John's road.*

15   BIG APPLE BITES BACK

I got sick of just reading about people doing this –
all kinds of epic journeys. ... You never really go out
and do it. But really all you need is a chunk of change and
the time.

John Carr, walking
The Appalachian Trail.

****

With melancholy, I left Sag Harbor for The Big
Apple. I had promised my neighbor, a huge
baseball fan, that I would park my rig outside
new Yankee Stadium for a photo. The vow was easier to

make than fulfill. The reality of maneuvering a truck camper rig through New York City proved daunting.

Brooklyn is where I lost it. At the end of the day, the home of the Bronx Bombers might as well have been in Rangoon. Cruising the Long Island Expressway proved easy. With my oversized Rand McNally Atlas and trusty GPS, the problem was not getting lost, but getting *somewhere.*

The closer I drew to New York City, the more I became Dennis Weaver in the TV series *McCloud.* The story line was a NYC police detective who was actually a cop transplanted from Taos, New Mexico. In the credits, he rides a horse through New York City down the skyscraper canyons of Manhattan. The juxtaposition was similar to the Clampetts in Beverly Hills in a jalopy.

My 2008 GMC Sierra truck was not a jalopy. Virtually new, it sparkled in ebony paint with proud red "GMC" letters in front and rear. My custom-built, ten-foot Wolverine camper was a scant four months old. Not a ding, all systems operating perfectly.

I had negotiated Chicago, Detroit, and Cleveland with no sense of being out of place. But New York City is, well, *New York City.* A teaming hubbub of five boroughs that seem scatter-connected by freeways, expressways, throughways, bridges, ferries, and did I mention – tunnels?

Thirty years ago, I had traveled through by car and had been surrounded by the cacophony of honking yellow taxis. New York had since instituted a stiff fine for any cabdriver needlessly blasting his horn. Streets were quieter, but no less busy.

Cruising west on Sunrise Highway, Route 27, at mid-morning, traffic grew more hectic by the minute. Passing through Islip and Massapequa, I had no preplanned route to Yankee Stadium. No planning guaranteed doom. The closer I got to Manhattan, the farther it receded and the higher my anxiety grew.

Unlike John Steinbeck, who got lost in New York City at the end of his journey, and had to enlist the help of a NYC cop, my GPS told me exactly where I was.

Via Freeport, Rockville Centre, and Valley Stream, I arrived in Brooklyn and came unglued. Traffic lanes increased. Brooklyn ensnared me like a Neil Simon play gone berserk. Signs on the left and right pointed to familiar icons: Aqueduct Race Track, JFK Airport, Coney Island, Brighton Beach, and Flatbush Avenue. I knew all those places, but still I did not exactly feel like a Lord of Flatbush.

I wanted to get onto the Shore Belt Parkway, but signs screamed *No Trucks Allowed.* Did that mean my truck, any truck, semi-trucks? What did it mean?

There were height limitations on various streets as well. Some said eleven feet, some twelve, some thirteen. I bypassed them religiously to avoid a low-hanging beam opening my camper like a sardine can.

My nerves swept my mind's radar. Yankee Stadium did not emerge as a reachable blip on the screen. I wanted out of Brooklyn and I could see people looking at my out-of-place rig as I negotiated Linden Boulevard, Flatbush Avenue, and then Ocean Avenue. The entire time in New York City, I never saw another pickup truck and camper.

Nowhere was the place I was getting to – fast. It would take a Woody Allen flick to rescue me from my New York angst. I drove on seeking an escape route from Brooklyn.

Signs screamed: *No trucks allowed. Buses Only. Height Restriction: 11'10".* *No Stopping or Parking by Order of NYPD.*

Ocean Avenue blended into Prospect Expressway. Exactly then, Yankee Stadium passed from my itinerary. I coulda, woulda, shoulda gotten off the Prospect Expressway where it merged with I-278 and gone deeper into New York City. I could have taken I-478 to the Brooklyn Battery Tunnel. Could have negotiated East River Drive, I-95, I-87 and arrived at Yankee Stadium.

Derek Jeter drove to Yankee Stadium, why couldn't I? Surely Alex Rodriguez didn't have a chauffeur take him to every game. TV production trucks and fan buses got to Yankee Stadium. Why couldn't I?

I could have gotten my picture taken outside the billion-dollar baseball palace and seen old Yankee Stadium nearby. I did none of the above. Instead, I punted.

The relative security of New Jersey beckoned. Where I could have headed to baseball's cathedral, I angled left toward the Gowanus Expressway, then the Shore Parkway, and paid ten dollars for the Verrazano Narrows Bridge toll to Staten Island.

At the apex of the bridge, I looked over to cloudy misty Manhattan. Somewhere was the Statue of Liberty, David Letterman preparing for his evening show, or the Philadelphia Phillies dressing for batting practice.

●●▶●●●●●●▶●●●●●▶●●●●●▶●●●●●▶●●●●●▶●●●●●▶●●●●●▶●●

Somewhere was Yankee Stadium. Damned Yankee Stadium. I applied a Yogi Berra one-liner he once said of a night spot: *No one goes there anymore. It's too crowded.*

This McCloud was riding his horse, not in Manhattan but toward the Goethals Toll Bridge and another ten dollar toll.

Shortly, I jammed down I-95, through Linden, Carteret and South Plainfield. I bypassed Philadelphia like a bad dream. They could have handed out new one-hundred dollar bills at every toll plaza to coax me into Philly and I would have plowed on. Big cities and I were done. I wanted wide-open Montana or the long cornfields of Wisconsin. My nerves needed settling.

At a toll booth, I asked the collector the most unusual thing he'd seen from travelers passing through.

"The usual. People having sex."

I decided there was nothing *usual* about the roads around New York City and Philly. A storm whipped rain and wind. By evening, I was in Gettysburg, Pennsylvania in a wooded campground surrounded by ghosts of the Civil War.

As I lay in bed, the nightmare passage through New York City still fresh, I did not ponder the World Series. The storm and rain abated. The evening turned quiet. In the dark and hush, a branch crackled and a bush rustled.

"Brownie, is that you out there?"

****

In the morning, I paid for a CD that gives a windshield tour of Gettysburg National Battlefield. I had been through

Gettysburg 40 years before on a high school trip and found the old Howard Johnson Motel where I had stayed.

That night, miles from Gettysburg in Winchester, Virginia, I pulled into a Walmart and was astounded. Since leaving home in September, the number of RVs hunkered down at Walmarts had dwindled. Many times in recent weeks, I had been the only RV present; however, in Winchester there were nineteen rigs. Among the monstrous bus-like RVs, I parked as a minnow among sharks. So many generators hummed, it sounded like the moments before a NASCAR race.

The next morning, the RV army had vanished – like a brigade off to war. In future days, the RVs were not present again. Only me. Why had there been so many in Winchester?

I found the answer in *The Winchester Star* which I had purchased on arrival, but didn't read until days later.

The night of the RV army, Willie Nelson had been in Winchester for a concert at the opening of a Patsy Cline museum. Winchester is Cline's birthplace. Willie Nelson's legion of fans explained all the RVs.

I love Willie's music. I might have scrounged a ticket. From that day forward, when I bought a newspaper, I scanned it that day. I didn't want to be surrounded by nineteen RVs and be clueless.

****

After Pennsylvania, I began a gentle drive toward the Great Smoky Mountains, ready for the Deep South's languid manners.

On the advice of both Carl Bernstein and a *Sag Harbor Express* reporter, I hit the Skyline Drive. It promised 110 miles of vistas, thirty-five mph speed limits, and total absence of signage, trucks, taxis and stress. The cost was fifteen dollars. The natural environment? Priceless.

Just a few miles along the high ridges of Virginia, I passed a young man on a bike. He was bearded, skinny, and disheveled. A road warrior on two wheels. I angled back to strike up a conversation.

"Been on the road awhile?"

"Since June from Maine. I'm walking the entire Appalachian Trail. Won't be at the end until Christmas if I'm lucky."

His name was John Carr, a student at the University of Tennessee – Chattanooga.

"How far you going?"

"Springer Mountain, Georgia, end of the trail."

"How long have you been planning the trip, couple years?"

"No. Just since February this year. I offered the idea to some people, but they couldn't find six months to take off. So I just took a semester off college."

"Exactly where and when did you start?"

"June 27, right outside Millinocket, Maine. The whole thing is 2,178 miles. I've gone about 1,250 so far."

John was not spending every night under the stars. He had friends and relatives along the way where he stayed, did laundry, and showered.

"Have you been interviewed before?"

"No. But I keep my friends informed through Facebook. I

send photos and stories when I get access to a computer once a month or so."

The day I met him, John was on a bike for the first time. An outfitter in a nearby town lent him a $900 bike to ride.

Talking to John for just minutes, it was obvious he was smart, driven, disciplined.

"Why are you doing this John?"

"There are so many reasons. I needed a break from school. But now I miss the hell out of going to school and I can't wait to get back. I got sick of just reading about people doing this – all kinds of epic journeys. They are supposed to be inspiring. But you read the book and put it back on the coffee table. You never really go out and do it. But really all you need is a chunk of change and the time."

"Have you had a day when you wanted to quit?"

"I've met kids and they quit hiking because it wasn't what they expected. Maybe they just had a really bad day. I didn't come out here thinking it was going to be all lollipops and gumdrops. I've had times where at the end of the day, I asked what the hell am I doing out here? But usually it just takes a good night's sleep. Never make a decision at the end of a day. Because you will decide something stupid. Just sleep on it. If you are having bad days every day, just quit."

John carried a cell phone.

"I do have to call my Mom once in a while to tell her I'm OK. She was completely against this trip. She was afraid if I took time off from school, I wouldn't go back."

"What about your Dad?"

"He passed away when I was little."

181

●●▶●●●●●▶●●●●●▶●●●●●▶●●●●●▶●●●●●▶●●●●●▶●●●●●▶●●

"I get the feeling there are more reasons you are out here."

"Sorta. I hesitate to call it spiritual, because I'm not really religious. I will say one of my best friends was killed in a car accident in January. My friend Max. That completely destroyed me. I ended up dropping out of school. So walking for six months gives you a lot of time to think. I find myself talking to him. It's funny. It's nice. You are out in the woods alone and I'll just talk to him."

"So what would you say to someone who is thinking about doing this?"

"By and large, it's life changing. It's the first time I have been on my own, free of responsibility. You are essentially, absolutely free. You don't want to be rushed. You are out here to get away from that."

That was fully revealed when John talked about his daily rations.

"To make things easy, I eat the same thing every day. I do a bagel and cream cheese for breakfast and Pop Tarts. For lunch I have chicken in a pouch."

"Will you ever eat chicken again back in the world?"

"I dunno. And every night for dinner it's macaroni and cheese. You are burning so many calories, that you can't get enough. That's why I'm losing so much weight. When I started out weighing 140 pounds, that window was already tight."

"What is your budget for the whole trip?"

"You can do it for $1,000, but you really can't stay anywhere. The total I am looking at after six months is around $5,000."

His possessions were spartan. A one-man tent, a sleeping bag and pad. A few books.

"My buddies think I'm insane because I carry too much weight. Normally my pack weighs between forty and forty-five pounds. Some of my buddies are hiking with thirty to thirty-five pounds."

"So what do you do with the books? Do you jettison them?"

"Oh no, I can't do that with a book. I have to either give it to someone who will appreciate it, or send it to someone who'll appreciate it. So even after I finish a book, I'll carry it until I can get it to a Post Office."

"What book are you reading right now?"

"*Nausea* by Jean-Paul Sartre."

My view of John improved from its already high level. A man, who licks mac and cheese off his lips nightly, then reads existentialists, you have to like a guy like that.

"Next on the list is *Siddhartha* by Hermann Hesse."

"You're reading pretty deep books. So what have you learned about yourself on the trip?"

"When you are younger, you just kind of wander through your life. Everything is set out for you. It's high school, college, find a job. It's kind of the rhythm I was stuck in. I heard about the Appalachian Trail when I was sixteen, but never thought I would do it. You are not going to be what you want to be if you sit on your ass and take classes in college which you might think will be interesting. And then get a job for a little while to get by and you end up getting stuck in that. I've met people on the trail who hated their jobs and said 'to hell with it.' They quit their jobs, sold their cars, gave up their apartment and came out here to get away. They figure out what they actually want to do and when they get back – they do it. It's insanely liberating."

John pulled out a cigarette. A Pall Mall.

"That's the worst of the worst," I said.

"No, it's the cheapest of the cheap."

Sucking in a few hydrocarbons gave John a second wind on his philosophy of life. As cars whizzed by, my tape recorder whirred. His smoke circles drifted into the clear Virginia air as John waxed eloquently.

"We've gotten to this point where people don't help each other out. But the Trail creates a trail community. Anyone out here has to have the time off and the funds to do it. So these towns know hikers and know we are insane for doing this. But we are all fairly nice kids and harmless and very easy to please. If you offer us a place on your floor to sleep and a hot shower, we will fall in love with you. This kind of thing doesn't exist anywhere else. You don't find that sort of hospitality from people."

"Did any animals bother you?"

"The most frightening one was a black bear that followed me about two miles. It smelled the food in my pack. It was in Pennsylvania. He was probably twenty feet away. I've seen six or seven bears so far."

"What are you going to do, the day after you finish the trail?"

"Well when you are out on the trail for a few days, you definitely start craving. But you're on a budget. So it would be pizza. Steak would be great. Maybe lobster."

"Is there anything I can do to help out?"

"Well you could lighten my load. Mind taking my pack someplace up the line?"

We broke out a map and picked a place called Elkwallow Rest Area. He gave me his backpack with his entire trail-worthy possessions. His *Siddhartha* and Sartre. His mac and cheese. His seven-ounce bags of chicken.

"John, you are a trusting soul. I could grab this bag and you'd never see me or it again."

"It's just stuff."

Perfect existentialism from a kindred spirit, doing at twenty-one what I was at fifty-seven. Chucking convention, carving time, raising cash and heading out.

Down the road, I found Elkwallow and talked the attendant into hiding John's pack behind a wood pile. Several hours later, John Carr found it waiting for him.

That's life on the Appalachian Trail.

Godspeed John Carr.

****

At the start of Skyline Drive, I was in the East. When I got off near Afton, Virginia, all the signs referred to the Rockville Gap. I had transformed to the South. On a high hill, I saw a rusty, creaking water tank. A decrepit, abandoned gas station had last pumped fuel when it was one dollar a gallon. Shuttered motels and junk cars completed the snapshot.

The town of Afton didn't look like an overnighter, so I moved on to Waynesboro, Virginia, found my trusty Walmart and settled in.

Out walking later, I heard bugle calls, the rat-a-tat of drums. I watched from a distance as cadets at Fishburne Military Academy pulled down the flag at exactly six thirty p.m. and then marched away, perhaps forty strong, with drummers at the rear.

****

The distant call for me was toward Abingdon, Virginia – the town where John Steinbeck abandoned his journey fifty years ago. Can any good thing come out of Abingdon? I found the answer, but then only questions at a Tennessee church where the congregation ate live worms.

Film at eleven – *down John's road.*

16 THE DEEP SOUTH

After Abingdon, nothing.

> John Steinbeck, at the
> emotional end of his
> journey in Virginia.

****

Side-slipping Roanoke and Blacksburg, Virginia, I rolled into Abingdon on a cool Halloween afternoon. This Virginia city of 8,000 was a stop I had carefully planned. In 1960, Steinbeck essentially assigned Abingdon to the grainy sidelines. He kicked it to an exit ramp and virtually declared his journey at end:

●●▶●●●●●▶●●●●●▶●●●●●▶●●●●●▶●●●●●▶●●●●●▶●●

It is very strange. Up to Abingdon, Virginia, I can reel back the trip like film. I have almost total recall, every face is there, every hill and tree and color, and sound of speech and small scenes ready to replay themselves in my memory. After Abingdon, nothing.

Rereading *Travels with Charley* left me wondering. Of all the cities between New Orleans and New York City, why had he given up in Abingdon? What did he miss there? Seeking atonement for Abingdon, I began poking around.

Abingdon agreed with me at first glance and last. It had historical *essence*. It had the grandiose Martha Washington Inn/Hotel and across the street The Barter Theater. Several museums, the Chamber of Commerce and *The Abingdon Virginian* newspaper were all closed Saturday. But I could not wait until Monday to find Abingdon's redeeming social value.

At a visitor information center I asked about senior citizen centers, hoping to find a sharp-minded denizen. My question to him or her would be simple? What did John Steinbeck miss by leaving Abingdon in his taillights?

Outside the low-slung senior center I was referred to, a message board announced: "Bridge Today." Inside, two dozen people shuttled between tables in a rotating ensemble.

As play concluded, I asked an organizer if someone with the gift of gab might provide a primer on 1960 Abingdon. He pointed out a retired educator and a former coal executive. I begged for twenty minutes and pulled out my recorder.

Pauline "Blue" Gotham, the retired teacher/administrator,

was nervous, mentally pacing. Already looking quite elegant, she only had fifteen minutes to spare.

"I've got a date to prepare for."

When Gene Matthis, the retired coal manager, saw Steinbeck's book, he gleamed.

"You've got my favorite Steinbeck, *Travels with Charley*. I love that book. Wasn't Charley kind of a wimp? And didn't Steinbeck talk his wife into joining him at some swanky Chicago Hotel."

"Right on both counts, Gene. How old are you?"

"I'm eighty-one."

"I don't dare ask a southern belle how old she is, do I?"

"I don't care. I'm seventy-seven."

I asked Blue what Steinbeck had missed.

"He would have seen the Barter Theater. It has been here since the Thirties right there on Main Street. He would have seen the Martha Washington Inn. It's been here even longer. In the 1960s, those were very much in operation."

I pled ignorance on The Barter.

"It was started in the depression by a man named Robert Porterfield. He was in the theater arts business and grew up in Washington County. Actors were starving to death during the depression. So they started the theater with farmers bringing in produce to get a seat."

I asked if Steinbeck could have seen a show in November 1960.

"Well, it was seasonal in those days. It is not now. Those days, the season would have closed in September."

I asked Gene what he had been doing in fall 1960.

"I had my nose stuck in the coal mines from daylight to dark. I spent a lot of time in the bowels of the earth. I was general manager of a coal company. They started you young back in those days. I retired in 1991."

"He was high up," Blue blurted, "an executive."

"What were you doing in 1960 Blue?"

"I was a teacher."

"What grades?"

"I taught them all. In 1960 I was probably at John Battle High School."

"Blue, did the boys drive up and down Main Street in Chevys with cigarettes rolled up their T-Shirt sleeves?"

"Most of the time the kids went over to Bristol (Tennessee). There was not that much going on here. There was more action in Bristol. They had fast food places already. Football was big too. Everyone turned out for the football games. We didn't have a movie theater. If you had a date, you went to the movie theater in Bristol. "

"Where did everyone work, Gene?"

"In coal. They would all commute. Abingdon in those days was kind of a bedroom town for coal people."

According to Blue, coal was a furtive word in 1960.

"Really and truly, people in Abingdon didn't acknowledge the coal fields much. I came here from Richmond when I was twenty years old. You'd say something about coal mines or coal fields, and they'd say, 'whaa-aaaay, we don't have any coal in Abingdon, darling.'"

"Were there factories?" I asked.

"There was a Harwood Manufacturing company, where

they made shirts, I think. There was a bunch of sewing machines lined up and the ladies went in there and just sewed away."

"Was there anybody famous that came from Abingdon?"

"Well we did have the Barter Theater. Ernie Borgnine got his start here. Patricia Neal got her start here. Gregory Peck and Robert Mitchum played here. They would all come here as young actors with stars in their eyes."

"So that was a big deal, Blue, if Gregory Peck was in town."

"No, it would not have been. He was nobody then. He didn't get big until years later."

"He was in the Little Leagues here," Gene added.

"Did those young handsome actors win the hearts of all the local Abingdon girls?"

"Most of the parents in town wouldn't let their girls date the Barter guys. They were from New Yaaaaaark, or places like that."

There was a trend forming. Blue elongated words she felt were important.

Blue said plays based on Steinbeck books had been performed at the Barter, including *The Grapes of Wrath* and *Of Mice and Men.*

"Let's wrap this up, Blue. You have a date waiting. If Steinbeck had arrived on a Saturday at five p.m., what would he have seen?"

"He could have driven all the way through town and not seen anybody. If he'd have gotten here at five o'clock on a Saturday evening, the streets would have been rolled up."

"Blue, do a sell job. Convince John Steinbeck to stop in Abingdon. There must be a reason."

"The people, the natives of southwest Virginia, and Abingdon, are the finest people I have ever known. Their work ethic is unbelievable. When I was a principal, I would not hire a secretary unless they came from Abingdon or southwest Virginia somewhere. The people themselves are just wonderful and I think he would have had a good time."

"How about you, Gene? Convince Steinbeck to stay awhile."

"I would tell him, you missed a damn good play at The Barter. Intellectually, he would have been very comfortable with Robert Porterfield and all those people who played at The Barter. I think from day one, this town has been sort of an intellectual oasis in an otherwise dreary desert."

Blue rolled her eyes at that hyperbole, and darted off to her date. Gene had a little more time. We went outside and I took a photo of him next to my rig.

****

NASCAR calls the south home. As I left Abingdon for good, I saw a sign for Bristol Motor Speedway and took a look.

The stadium seats 180,000 spectators around a half-mile oval. Imagine trying to cram a dinner party for forty around a folding card table. That's what the place feels like. At the gargantuan stadium, not a soul was in sight. No security guards and no padlocks. The gate to the infield apron and track splayed wide open. I could have driven Gabilan down to the high-speed oval and taken a lap or two. No one would have noticed.

For a second I thought of doing it. But the extremely banked oval and windy conditions at the base of the track kicked in my common sense.

****

On a rainy road, I drove to Morrisville, Tennessee and ate at an International House of Pancakes. With a dozen restaurants nearby, I chose IHOP for one reason. Research revealed it was a franchise on the rise in 1960 America.

Sunday morning looking for a church, I found several, but none had reader boards announcing services. Odd for an industry trying to recruit. Why not put Hours of Operations out front?

Finally I found a storefront church. Musicians unloaded guitars and drums. One member waved, a friendly enough gesture for me to ask when services began.

"Ten thirty."

"I'll be back."

When I returned, a congregation of perhaps eighty was seated around tables in a medium-sized, strip mall store. Balloons floated over most chairs. The young pastor's elderly mother told me: "We do things unorthodox here, but we don't do snake charming or anything like that."

Maybe not snake charming, but close.

The pastor had been teaching on fear. Today's concluding

message featured three people who had been through a series of *Fear Factor* challenges. Today someone would win $100 in the concluding challenge. The task? The first person to eat eight live worms would win the C-note.

Ah, church in the Bible Belt. Only a man named Nick accepted the challenge. The other contestants stared at the eight worms and granted them a pardon. Not Nick, who not only ate the worms, but chewed them with gusto. People hid behind their Bibles, unable to look. He won the $100.

"My wife and I are planning a trip and we could use the money," Nick said.

The church was called The Connection. The service returned to more or less Protestant vanilla. Lots of loud music, testimonies, and skits. At the end, worm eaters and non-worm eaters wrote their fears on the balloons which were taken outside and released.

"Your fear is on the outside and inside of that balloon," a pastor's assistant said. "Watch that balloon until it goes into the clouds. That is where God is ready to accept your fear."

Two men around my table, in their bravado, refused to admit to fears of any kind. A third man, James, noted his fear of flying. On my balloon, I wrote a couple of garden-variety fears and watched as it drifted skyward and soon out of sight.

****

Then I hit the road with Georgia on my mind. I wanted to visit the man, a general contractor, from whom I had bought my truck in early spring. I had found a brand-new carpenter's square behind seats in the cab and wanted to return it. We went to lunch.

Bruce always asks interesting questions.

"Do you have more or less faith in America now that you have made this trip?"

"I always had faith, Bruce. I never lost that. It neither increased nor decreased. What I have found on the trip so far is that people have more faith in themselves to get us out of this economic mess than they have in politicians. Some trust Obama, some trust Congress. Most just trust themselves."

Five months earlier when I had bought the truck Bruce had invited me to his office. Deep, red woods and leather chairs made the den feel like the lair of a man just back from African safari.

"It feels comfortable, Bruce. Like two old friends talking about the last lion, or wildebeest shot on the Serengeti. Perhaps they are enjoying an expensive Cognac."

That was pure fluff from me. I can never remember drinking Cognac in my life, but think I know what people feel like when drinking it.

To Bruce and anybody who would listen, I continued to share my fear of New Orleans. Bruce flashed another highly probing question.

"What is the greatest fear you have ever had, John?"

The answer lay in the terror of the dark I had as a boy. My father, in a misguided attempt to cure me of the fear, only made it worse.

He tried to force the fear out of me by leaving a yard light on after sunset. My task was to turn the yard light off by

forcing a long walk to the switch located in the barn farthest
from our house.

It terrified me and became an ongoing nightmare. Great
hordes of men waited to kidnap me. Panting wild animals on
the loose prowled to dismember me. Pure strangers fought
over the right to pull me into outbuildings and beat me
bloody. This was my nightly crucible. The distance seemed
interminable.

Walking in semi-darkness toward the barn was not so bad.
After all, my chore was to turn off the light. Once the light
was off, the return journey came in pitch-black terror. The
distance became 100 times greater.

I would race at the speed of light toward home, my heart
ramming like a piston. Lance Armstrong's heart never
pumped more blood. It was pure and simple agony.

Twenty-five years later, after moving off that farm, I
returned for a visit. Looking down the driveway toward the
barn, I felt ashamed; or so I told the man who asked the
original question.

"The distance seemed so short, Bruce. I felt ridiculous. I
had turned a walk of perhaps thirty seconds, in my child's
mind, into a crossing of the Atlantic Ocean."

Then Bruce asked something interesting, something even
more intriguing.

"What was the true distance to the yard light?" Bruce
inquired, steering me toward a different answer: The distance
might not be measured in feet, but in fear.

Was it the short distance of my adulthood? Or the yawning
dangerous trek my father had demanded of me as a

frightened child? Bruce set my thinking totally on edge.

Since then I have often pondered the answer. What is the true measure of any distance? Is it measured by emotion or by a simple tape measure? It seems logical that several factors collided in determining the true distance to that yard light so many years ago.

I began thinking of my Steinbeck journey based on Bruce's premise. In my travels from Washington to Maine and now back home again, was it just 12,000 miles? Was it simply a big black GMC truck passing through the day and night, its odometer clicking off the miles?

Or was it something much more complex? I've come to believe my trip was actually the sum total of every mile I have ever traveled overlaid on those 2009 miles.

Whatever the answer, it was time to test New Orleans, a city I feared. Was my fear real or myth? Time would tell – *down John's road.*

****

I began my civil rights research long before New Orleans in Anniston and Selma, Alabama. In those cities, most Black Americans extended a hand of friendship and answered any probing question. Others would not give the time of day.

17   HEADING TO NEW ORLEANS

You know, if injustice is being done to just one person,
it is being done to us all. That's what I believe.

George, retired Marine,
Selma, Alabama.

****

The refrains of sad songs about New Orleans filled my mind as I drove south into a strange land. Not least were *Mr. Bojangles* by Nina Simone or *Walking to New Orleans* by Fats Domino.

●●▶●●●●●▶●●●●●▶●●●●●▶●●●●●▶●●●●●▶●●●●●▶●●●●●▶●●

Born and raised in the Midwest, eight years in the Navy worldwide, and the past two decades on Puget Sound, left the Deep South seeming like another planet. Mars perhaps.

Yet I am also a child of the 1960s, having watched the civil rights movement unfold nightly on Walter Cronkite's *CBS Evening News.* I know about the South, but hardly experienced its racial history.

New Orleans evoked anxiety that convinced me I was a closet racist. Was it lack of courage, knowledge or unfamiliarity? Was it flat out bigotry? At age fifty-seven, I was afraid of New Orleans. The things I thought about New Orleans, before ever visiting, embarrass me now.

They were not without history. My father-in-law left the Navy in 1963 after twenty years. Doing so, he gave up a large chunk of pension by refusing shore duty in New Orleans. He hated the place. In the mid-1990s I worked with a man who once lived and worked in New Orleans. He claimed he would never return, even if it meant poverty elsewhere.

New Orleans had a hold on me, but it was all based on what other people said, or on television and media reports. To break this negative hold, I would have to see New Orleans myself.

****

Before arriving in New Orleans in early November, I chugged through the Mid-South, then Deep South. Where a line separates the two, I did not know. Perhaps near Anniston, Alabama.

One morning, insomnia led me to leave Anniston hours ahead of normal departure. Downtown, a sign pointed toward the Martin Luther King Jr. Pavilion. I drove past and found an oversized gazebo and small stage in a block-square park. I searched my memory for what Cronkite might have said about this city.

The 1960s? Martin Luther King? Anniston, Alabama? Did something happen here? Did someone get shot? Did MLK give a speech here, get arrested, and organize a sit-in?

My mind was blank. I circled the gazebo-pavilion looking for plaques and found none. It was just after eight a.m. Two middle-aged black women walked laps in the park. Their slow, deliberate pace looked post-surgery and doctor-ordered. It wasn't exercise. Their heads were straight down. They looked pained, immersed in deep thought. They talked little, stopping often as the older woman used a cell phone.

On one of their passes by my rig, I ventured in.

"Excuse me, could I ask a question?"

The younger woman stopped. The older woman slowed, but walked on. Both eyed my big truck with Washington state plates.

Who the heck is this out-of-state, middle-aged white man? Or so they must have thought.

"This Pavilion seems to be named after Dr. Martin Luther King. Did he give a speech here or something?"

The woman who had stopped opened her mouth set to answer. She looked at the older woman, who kept walking, but did the talking.

"I dunno."

"Did Dr. King ever pass through here? Did something happen right here?"

"I don't know nothing 'bout no Martin Luther King in Anniston."

You could sense her mentally tugging her friend to keep walking. The stopped woman looked me in the eyes. Alone, I believe she would have talked. But the other woman's powerful sway was more persuasive than my question. Both women walked away.

Only later did I learn on May 14, 1961, Anniston was the site of the bombing, torching and beatings of passengers on a Greyhound bus during integration attempts by Freedom Riders.

Later in 1965 in Anniston, for the first time in the civil rights era, a white man was convicted of murdering a black man. Anniston did indeed have a racial history. The MLK Pavilion was not for decoration.

Skirting Montgomery, Alabama, I drove toward Selma, a town I recalled more clearly. My mind said there was an arched, concrete bridge and civil rights marches. There were hoses, horses and blood.

On Selma's outskirts, signs pointed to a Civil Rights Interpretive Center. Pulling into a mostly empty parking lot, a guide said a short movie was just beginning. Then he recommended a self-guided tour. In the theater were three black people – two women and a man.

After the movie which depicted history in the area, I

approached the black man.

"Were you in the civil rights marches shown in the movie?"

"No. But I think my girlfriend Dorothy (pointing to one woman) took part. I was in Vietnam serving my country. I spent twenty-two years in the Marines. It was a good career."

Later, I apologized for what whites had done to blacks depicted in the movie. He seemed surprised.

"You don't have to be sorry. You weren't here. You didn't do nothing. You know, even the people that was here, I don't blame that much either. They didn't know any better."

"You mean you're not upset for the evil stuff that went on in 1960s America and before?"

"You have to know what evil is. You have to identify it, before you can attack it. They didn't think what they were doing was evil. I'm not forgiving them mind you. I'm just saying they didn't know they were doing evil."

"What about now?"

"Things are getting better all the time. Little by little, things is getting better. You know, if injustice is being done to just one person, it is being done to us all. That's what I believe."

His name was George. He lived in South Carolina.

His girlfriend Dorothy was not talkative. No matter how I phrased or rephrased questions, she evaded.

We lazed our way to the front door. George had one last thing to say.

"You see those white people in that movie? You see their pictures on the wall in there? I'm talking about the white people that walked with the blacks that stood beside them. Their life was hell. In some ways it was worse than the black folks. They knew what to expect. Once you were a white person who came out on the side of civil rights, your life got a whole lot worse. A helluva lot worse."

It seemed a magnanimous position for a middle-aged black man in America to take. I shook his hand and said goodbye.

In the parking lot was a more elderly security guard. I didn't have to strike up a conversation with him. He came to me.

His name was Kirk. He lived in nearby Lowndes County and fully remembered Selma in 1965.

"You were how old in 1965?"

"I was born March 20, 1925."

"Up to that time had you never voted? Had you never tried to register?"

"Not before the march."

"Were you a part of that first march on the bridge in February 1965 when the cops did all that stuff?"

"I was out there."

"Did you get smacked?"

"I did. Me and my wife and kids. We didn't know nothing. We were standing out there and we were just looking at the march. Then they had those horses and everything, running all over the people. Me and my wife were just standing there. They came over and said 'Get the hell back in the car.'"

"Did you get back in the car?"

"We had to. Because if you didn't, you know, they had those sticks. They was going to beat you with those sticks.

203

We had no choice. They ran into my car with a horse. The man came by on the horse and held my door and said 'Get back in that car.' Before I could get back in the car, the horse hit the door and bent it. I had a Ford. The horse kicked a dent in, but they never did anything about it."

"You were there with your wife and several of your kids."

"Yah, right. I think I had five kids at the time."

"So then momentum built for the big march?"

"Oh yah. Martin Luther King left Montgomery to come out here."

"So the big march, the really big one was in March 1965 and your family went the whole way?"

"No, not the kids. Just my wife. I took off from work. The march was about three days and the weather was not good. There was a tent city right here," he said pointing to a corner of the parking lot.

"So the march grew in size each day?"

"It just kept getting bigger and bigger. People was coming from all over."

Kirk remembered seeing Dr. King, Ralph Abernathy and a "skinny" Jesse Jackson. The marchers presented a petition to Alabama Governor George Wallace, who accepted it. Kirk never saw Wallace because of the crush of people.

"Did you feel you were doing something important?"

"I knew it was a big thing."

Kirk worked construction for fifty years. He and his wife had thirteen children. Three were stillborn, leaving six boys and four girls.

"Some are in the Army, the service. Some have college

degrees. I never figured that I would be alive to see that. But the Lord allowed me to see that. He sure did."

"You said things are getting better in America for blacks. What needs to get better, faster?"

"If I was Obama, I'd think that people need more housing and better housing. Living conditions. We can all be living a little better."

"So if you worked in construction for fifty years, you can drive all around and look at stuff you built. You probably built buildings that have already been knocked down."

"Well up in Montgomery, there would sure enough be stuff that I worked on. I used to leave from here every morning going to Montgomery. I've run that Montgomery Highway for fifty years."

"Do you and your wife go to church?"

"Me and my wife we go to Shiloh Baptist Church. That's right. The Bible is for reading. The whole thing. That's what I tell my kids. Don't let Him catch you with your work undone. You better be ready at all times."

There was something about the attitude of these two black men changing my view toward New Orleans. Both admitted much progress was needed in race relations in America, but did not seem bitter in the interim.

Continuing over the Edmund Pettus Bridge into Selma, the city looked downtrodden from any angle. Corners were peppered with Johnny-come-lately garages and used-tire sellers. Selma's poverty is institutional. Ashtabula, Ohio's poverty seemed situational. Ashtabula might rise from its predicament. Selma's predicament seemed final.

●●▶●●●●●●▶●●●●●▶●●●●●▶●●●●●▶●●●●●●▶●●●●●●▶●●●●●▶●●

****

I decided to make Meridian, Mississippi by nightfall. In the Navy, I had spent two months there in 1977 learning to type, file and be a Navy clerk. The town was the opposite of Selma: bustling, thriving, with big box stores, shopping malls, and franchise restaurants.

The next morning I drove Gabilan out to Meridian Naval Air Station to reminisce. With no military ID card or sponsor, I was flatly denied entry. Plaintively, I begged until the security guard stopped me cold.

"Listen. Did you ever hear of 9/11? Everything changed after that. You ain't getting in."

In 1977, the road to the base had been strewn with rickety houses with old sofas on porches. Disheveled cars with hoods up were everywhere. I remembered being shocked at the red-clay poverty in 1977. It was not nearly as prevalent on my 2009 trip to Meridian.

New Orleans' scent was in the air. Signs announced hotels and attractions in New Orleans. I parked in Slidell, Louisiana at an immaculate shopping mall.

Finally, I ended the fifteen-round fight I had waged with myself since the trip began. I vowed to drive straight into New Orleans the next morning. The devil of fear be damned.

If something happened – and odds were stratospherically against that – so be it.

****

I thought New Orleans would be a nemesis *down John's road*. But the nemesis was not fear, racism, or anxiety, but a hurricane. New Orleans has stopped being defined by Cajun food, French Quarter frivolity, or the beloved NFL Saints. In New Orleans, for the foreseeable future, it's going to be about Katrina.

18   INSIDE NOLA

*Let me tell you, I've read the whole Jack Kerouac and
everything. When you are out there and you think you
are king of the road, you're not. You're not king of
anything. Basically, you're homeless. Which I do not
like being for any length of time.*

New Orleans cabdriver
Robert M.

****

R eading about the devastation of New Orleans by
Katrina, the diaspora of residents and rampant crime
made me wary of the Crescent City.

The night before arriving in New Orleans, my retired Navy officer brother sent me an e-mail: *Be safe my brother. In all my thirty-two years in the Navy, traveling all over the world, I have never felt as unsafe as I had in New Orleans.*

The cascade of New Orleans warnings would never abate.

The next morning at a gas station, I talked one last time to my fears and approached a Louisiana State Police officer.

"Could I ask you a question, sir?"

"Fire away."

"I have the need today to drive into the middle of the Lower Ninth Ward in New Orleans on a book project. Friends and relatives say to avoid the Lower Ninth. Excuse me for my ignorance, but will I be safe there?"

"Hmmm. The Lower Ninth Ward in that rig? In the daytime, you'll be safe. In the nighttime, there are places you wouldn't want to go. For the most part, you'll be fine. It's not like Chicago, where you're at a stoplight and they mug you and steal your tires while you're sitting there."

Ouch. It hurts to be Chicago in that cop's eyes.

"I'm just going in, parking out front of a school, taking a photo and then I'm on my way. Will that be cool?"

"Don't do anything stupid. You don't want to stop where the good old boys are sitting on the porch or gas station drinking tons of beer. As long as you don't draw attention you'll be fine. In fact, there are some really, very nice parts to the Lower Ninth Ward."

My resolve had changed prior to the cop. The night before I had decided to act like a man. If that cop had told me to stay the hell out of the Lower Ninth, I still would have gone in.

●●▶●●●●●●●▶●●●●●▶●●●●●▶●●●●●▶●●●●●▶●●●●●▶●●●●●▶●●

****

New Orleans' skyline rose on the flat horizon – a skyline made familiar to Americans during Katrina. Research revealed a fairly swanky RV park at the edge of the French Quarter. I pulled in, arranged for a guided Hurricane Katrina bus tour and walked ten blocks to the Mississippi River waterfront.

The French Quarter attacks the senses. The temperature was rising to eighty degrees, and the aromas, sights and sounds of the Quarter wafted into the warm Louisiana morning.

It's a cordon of debauchery, replete with excess alcohol, trencherman eating and girls exposing breasts for beads during Mardi Gras. I came across sex bars. Hawkers grabbed at me coaxing me into live sex shows. It was all available and all before noon. It seemed more like Amsterdam's red-light district. But it really was Bourbon Street, one of America's most recognized thoroughfares.

History managed to seep through. Soaring cathedral bells, street jazz bands (some exquisitely good playing duct-taped instruments), and the clip-clop of horse carriages added to the cacophony.

The bus tour meandered throughout New Orleans. Our guide, a young man with a University of New Orleans Fine Arts degree, brimmed with facts. Among them was that New Orleans' population was 484,674 in 2000.

"Most estimates put it at 325,000 these days," said the guide. "We'll get a more accurate picture after the census of

2010." (In fact, the U.S. Census Bureau reported the population at 343,829 in its February 2011 report.)

The Lower Ninth Ward by bus was a puzzle. Devastation lived alongside reconstruction. In some blocks, half the homes looked abandoned forever. The other half stood proudly – either new, or rebuilt on stilts.

Unkempt lawns looked untouched since Katrina, others looked trimmed yesterday. Many homes had no lawn at all, just moldy junk piles.

Actor Brad Pitt's Make It Right Foundation had rebuilt "green" homes in the Lower Ninth. These small, unpretentious homes soared off ground level with true architectural flair.

During the tour, signs read: *One New Orleans. Rethink. Renew, Review.* The man hired by Mayor Ray Nagin as reconstruction czar departed the week I drove through. Whether Edward Blakely was axed, pushed out, or resigned was conjecture. His tenure proved controversial.

I asked our tour bus driver what rank-and-file residents thought of Blakely. The driver was raised in the Lower Ninth Ward. His opinion meant something.

"Sometimes they put people in power and then don't give them any power. Sometimes they put people in power who don't have any brains. Well brains, that's not something you can give a man. He has 'em or he doesn't."

Our bus driver negotiated his way through the tight Lower Ninth Ward with aplomb. Watching his technique, it was obvious I could not have navigated the tight streets and construction in the Lower Ninth in my camper rig.

211

●●▶●●●●●▶●●●●●▶●●●●●▶●●●●●▶●●●●●▶●●●●●▶●●●●●▶●●

I decided to call a taxi as John Steinbeck had done in his 1960 visit. I would have a hack find the school where Steinbeck witnessed the pungent racism of the "Cheerleaders" so richly described in *Travels with Charley*.

Plus, a cab driver would know the real New Orleans. In the morning, I asked the taxi dispatcher to send a black driver, if possible, to drive me to William Frantz Public School.

He sounded wary.

"Let me get this straight. You only want a black driver. You got a problem buddy?"

"No, this is serious. I'm going to William Frantz Public School to look around and take a photo. The school was the site of a famous racist episode in 1960. The writer John Steinbeck witnessed it and put it in his book *Travels with Charley*. It's a very famous scene."

"What's that got to do with you and a black driver?"

"I want to compare what happened then with what's going on now in race relations. It would just be better to have a black driver. I'm writing a book."

"Aren't we all, buddy? I've heard that before. All right, here's the deal. It's early in the morning, it's busy. I've got drivers all over the city. I'll see what I can do."

The cab arrived in just a few minutes. Out jumped the driver. Very much Louisianan. Very much white.

"I asked for a black driver. I guess it didn't work out?"

"I heard the call go out. There were black guys willing to do it, but too far away. The guys you really need are off today. I can put my soul hat on if you want me to."

"No, let's get going. I need the William Frantz Public

School in the Lower Ninth Ward, 3811 North Galvez Street."

"Gotcha."

To kill time in the cab, I began giving the driver my quick spiel on GMC truck, Wolverine Camper, John Steinbeck, 1960, etc., about halfway through his face lighted up in recognition.

"Oh yah, yah, yah. *Travels with Charley*, right?"

"Correct. There was this school and this little girl. I forgot her last name. It was Ruby Phillips or Ruby Billups, or …"

"Ruby Bridges," the hack said.

"So you're familiar with the incident and the spewing at the black girl?"

"I remember my Dad talking about it. I used to think, what barbarians these suckers are. How could they be so hateful? I used to take a dollar from my allowance and give it to the Civil Rights Club. It was only later that I came down here and saw for myself."

"You weren't born here?"

"I was born in Baton Rouge."

"How long have you worked as a cabbie in New Orleans?"

"Let's see – twenty-nine years."

"It's the only job I've ever had I don't hate. I mean truly hate."

He told me of many jobs traveling around the country before settling in Louisiana.

"Let me tell you, I've read the whole Jack Kerouac and everything. When you are out there and you think you are king of the road, you're not. You're not king of anything. Basically, you're homeless. Which I do not like being for any length of time."

"I guess I've been homeless since September 1 in my rig."

"Yah, but yours is a different kind. It's got a purpose."

"Where do you live?"

"In a place called Gentilly Terrace."

"Yes. I saw it on my Hurricane Katrina bus tour."

"It did not flood. It had berms. So the streets flooded, but the houses didn't."

I wanted to move the conversation toward racism, so I flat out broached it.

"I've been reading about this goofball Blakely in the paper and he claims there is going to be a race war in New Orleans in ten years or so?"

"That stupid son of a bitch. I'll tell you who the biggest racists are here. I call them the race pimps. They are the failed black leadership who blame everything on racism. They are the worst racists down here."

The cabbie grew profane and animated.

"I mean the worst. Blakely, Nagin. The Al Sharptons and Jesse Jacksons of the world, they are the biggest racists down here. I'm not saying we are not all guilty. But they are the worst. You know, it's their standard shtick. Racism, racism. How old are you? You look about my age."

"I'm fifty-seven," I said.

"You remember when being a commie was the worst thing you could be? Joe McCarthy and all that. Well now, if you want to destroy somebody, you call them a racist. It's devastating. It's character assassination."

His glib and persuasive rant had no end.

●●▶●●●●●▶●●●●●▶●●●●●▶●●●●●▶●●●●●▶●●●●●▶●●●●●▶●●

"It would be really interesting if I could live fifty or 100 more years and see what the buzz word is to destroy people at that time. Because I think racism is going to get old sooner or later and they'll have a new way to destroy people. Because that's just the way people are."

"Is Nagin going to get reelected?"

"He's gone. Term limiiiiiiiiiits," he pealed with satisfaction.

"I remember him during the Katrina coverage," I said. "He shoots from the hip."

"He doesn't care."

"And this guy Blakely that Nagin brought in," I said, "what kind of guy would talk about race war when his job is to bring the city together?"

"Basically, all his efforts are wasted. He's done all this work and said, 'piss on it.'"

I've been in enough taxis to know cabbies act like social gurus and psychiatrists. They are talking heads on four tires. They want you entertained, so you will tip higher. My driver was a gem and a verbal chameleon.

"So you were born in Baton Rouge, left at age ten, and traveled?"

"I landed in Connecticut," he said in pseudo-Brooklynese.

"How do you do that?"

"It depends on what kind of mood I'm in, or who I'm talking to. So how has your Rocinante been treating you?"

I was only semi-shocked to learn he knew the name of Steinbeck's original camper rig. This cabbie was no rube.

"You are one of those literary cab drivers."

215

"Not too many of us left. I just hate work. I like being out here. And getting rid of people fast, so you don't get stuck with 'em. Let me tell you. I've known some strange people."

"I hope I'm not strange, but I want to talk to people about race relations. Have they gotten better or worse?"

"Oh, they've gotten better. It's slowly getting better."

At that moment we pulled up to William Frantz Public School. It was closed and under renovation. On the front steps we took each other's photo. We walked around the grounds, his meter running at the curb. The hack talked about post-Katrina New Orleans.

"It's not a Studs Terkel kind of story with facts and facts. My deal with Katrina is kind of *Catch 22,* horrific, but bizarrely entertaining. I don't think too many people got it right. There's really a kind of surreal atmosphere about Katrina that is really black comedy people overlook. Someone should do an oral history of Katrina. When people get shaken up like that in Katrina, it was wildly amusing as well as destructive. People got scattered all over the country, and yet, all kinds of things still happened here. It was mesmerizing."

"Where were you living when it happened?"

"I was living here in the Lower Ninth."

"You're kidding. Right here? Let's go by your house. I'm willing to pay."

He did a casual California U-Turn in the road, drove the sidewalk, got honks from displeased drivers and we careened to his pre-Katrina home.

"What happened to you during Katrina?"

"It's funny. Take my guitars. I had twelve of them. Maybe one got damaged. I hung them up near the ceiling. I had twelve-foot ceilings and they were all up high."

He told me his house didn't have too much damage. Even though the water settled at five to seven feet deep, the cedar floors dried back to normal. Still he moved to Gentilly Terrace after Katrina.

"Were you one of the ones who stayed in the Lower Ninth during the storm?"

"No, I left because I didn't want to die. I believed them. I was running for my life."

"Where did you go?"

"I just went anywhere. I said, look, the first thing I gotta do is get out from underneath Lake Pontchartrain so I don't get flooded. So I went east. I'm going into Mississippi and a guy flags me down because I'm in the cab."

"I said, 'Look, you don't want to get in this cab.'"

"I was like an Okie on the run. Everything I owned was in there. I had two dogs and two cats."

My hack said the other guy claimed to be a Kansas City truck driver whose invalid mother was in Pass Christian, Mississippi. The guy got in and they drove east.

"So I get on the beach at Pass Christian and I saw the storm cloud. It looked like the clouds of the Dust Bowl – 50,000 feet of doom. If you would have seen night riders spewing through that cloud, it would not have struck as anything abnormal. It was like the fliers from hell. There were mountains of water. It looked awful."

He headed for Meridian, Mississippi until he heard Katrina

was too. He kept going.

"I ended up with a brother in Ohio and a sister in Chicago for awhile. I came back October 10."

"So you were gone a little over a month."

"I didn't want to leave. I mean I wanted to leave to save my life, but I wanted to come back quickly. It didn't work that way."

We pulled in front of his former Lower Ninth home.

"Look at that," he marveled. "It's been fully renovated."

****

Later, as we drove back to downtown New Orleans, the taxi driver explained why he has stayed in New Orleans and not moved elsewhere.

"The other thing about New Orleans is that it actually has a center. I guess that's a Spanish or French legacy, a town with a center. So many places in the Midwest, it's just a bundle of commercial activity. It's all for cars and everything goes whizzing around. There are skyscrapers, but if you look for a real downtown, it's really not there. The larger the city, the more commercial it is. There is not much walking. There are sidewalks, but cars come whizzing by so fast. It's alienating, demoralizing and very anti-social."

So there we were. New Orleans cabdriver with twenty-nine years under his chassis. Me with just seventy days under my own. I chimed in about life on the road.

"It's just big boxes. American cities are castles with moats, surrounded by big boxes. It's like feudal days. People are inside the boxes and the boxes are Walmart, Staples, Home Depot, and Lowes."

My cabbie was no big box fan, but gave them some credit.

"Well with a Walmart, that's a double-edged sword. It doesn't pay much wages, and puts people out of business, but especially for people on the edge, it's a major price savings."

I asked him about his other jobs.

"Everything I did, I couldn't stand. So I either got fired or quit. Payables clerk. Warehouse clerk. You name it. To me, work is a terrible way to spend your only life. You get thrown in with a bunch of people you can't stand to listen to. I don't see how most people do it. I mean you are supposed to love your job and all that, but who does?"

"I'd have to agree with you on that," I said.

"I just don't like to be part of an organization. It's all power struggles and the darker side of humanity. It's the boredom of your daily job. I just dunno."

"Well, I always liked my job as a journalist. It was something new. After all, it was the news. You weren't trying to sell the same insurance policy day after day."

"You were saved, definitely saved from the tedium," the cabdriver said.

We were back in downtown New Orleans when I decided to lighten conversation. No more racism, commercialism, communism, or any kind of -ism.

"So how many days a week you drive?"

"Four strong. I wasn't supposed to work today, but I heard this come over the radio, and I'm off and running."

"So it worked out for you and it worked out for me."

We pulled into the RV park with my pipsqueak truck camper next to fifty-foot, $500,000 RV buses.

"There it is," I said, proud of shiny black Gabilan.

"It's not that old. I guess I was expecting to see one identical to the one Steinbeck drove."

"You kidding me? A fifty-year-old truck and camper capable of going around the country? That would be hard to find."

"I suppose so."

We squared up the bill. It was about twenty-eight dollars – I gave thirty-five. I should have given him $100. His interview won my Best-of-Trip Award. Only at the very end did he give me his name.

"Bob."

"That's it?"

"Well, Robert. Robert M. He was reluctant to give me his last name. Instead he said, "You know, I've been thinking about some last thing to help your research."

I thought, it's coming. The home run. About New Orleans. The defining quote was near. He finally had something pithy to say on racism.

But what I got from Robert M. was what any New Orleans resident wants you to know today. All they can or will talk about is Hurricane Katrina.

"There's a real book about Katrina that hasn't been written. You would not believe the things that happened to the people when they left. The thing that is missing is the surreal side. Again, it was much closer to *M.A.S.H.* or *Catch 22* than it was to some total Greek tragedy. Because the most bizarre and amazing, crude slapstick things happened to people when they were uprooted."

"You mean the books out there are just facts?"

"The facts and the oh-this-is-so-terrible stuff. They missed the humanity of the whole thing, making it too one-dimensional. Too much of a polemic. Too bleak. There is an untold story. It's not as *Catch-22* right now, because life is settling down. There was all this Dr. Strangelove, crazy, wild, outside-the-box stuff, which nobody has really captured."

Robert M. could have been describing the Joads of *The Grapes of Wrath*. A band on the run. I considered Robert M. *a saint marching in* as he wheeled Cab 763 into a brilliant fall morning in New Orleans.

****

Leaving New Orleans, it smelled of *recovery*. Stain marks on buildings that revealed Katrina flood levels were fading. Cranes and construction barges ringed the city, building an improved levee system to staunch the next 100-year flood.

After checking out of the downtown RV park, only then did I see its extraordinary security. Unnoticed had been the eight-foot high concrete block walls with razor-like devices embedded at the top. Light poles were in each corner; several had security cameras. Perhaps I had not been as safe in New Orleans as I thought. Nevertheless, I took a celebratory lap around the Superdome, headed down Canal Street in bright sunshine and pointed to Houma, Louisiana.

As I left, the New Orleans Saints were undefeated and would eventually win the Super Bowl. Things definitely were getting easier in The Big Easy.

Arriving in Houma mid-afternoon, I walked down West Main Street, past Terrebonne Regional Medical Center and Terrebonne High School. I turned around and walked east until a small bayou and overhead bridge stopped me. Tucked among trees was the Terrebonne Parish Morgue. A delivery was being made.

****

In the distance was fabled Route 66, now just snatches of concrete, kitschy signs, and commerce bleeding John Steinbeck's *Mother Road* dry of tourist bucks. *Down John's road,* I nearly died on a blurry stretch of Interstate near Lake Charles, Louisiana.

After that, I was on Texas time.

19   THE HEART OF TEXAS

You know Texans. We like to think the sun rises and
sets on us. Well guess what? It doesn't.

Alan Henderson,
propane man in Texas.

****

I went inside Steinbeck's self-professed road weariness. After visiting Salinas and the Monterey Peninsula in 1960, one might believe Steinbeck was rejuvenated. It was not the case.

Old friends, haunts, and memories made him cut his trip

shorter. Crossing the Mojave Desert, Steinbeck wrote he only wanted to see two more places: Texas and a sample of the Deep South. Endless miles ceased to interest him.

I sat on the bed and stared into gray dreariness. Why had I thought I could learn anything about this land? For the last hundreds of miles, I had avoided people. Even at necessary stops for gasoline I had answered in monosyllables and retained no picture. My eye and brain had welshed on me.

I concocted my own theory on Steinbeck's *gray dreariness*. Steinbeck, the total Steinbeck, welshed on his own eyes and brain.

In 1960, he talked his wife into visiting him in Chicago at the ritzy Ambassador East Hotel. Martinis, no doubt, were served in The Pump Room. Elaine joined him in Seattle and drove the Pacific Coast with him. Finally, Elaine also joined him in Texas. With so much marital togetherness, on what grounds could the man claim loneliness?

True, I had daily e-mails and cell phone calls with my wife. They were hardly enough. For twenty-nine straight nights, I continued to sleep alone in Gabilan.

I stamp my claim on loneliness. I did not welsh on my trip.

****

In Louisiana, just after dusk between Houma and Lake Charles, something changed. It was a mystery at the time. I always looked forward to the hour just before and after sunset. The hours are purer, crisper and decision making is easier. I did not make trip decisions in the daytime hours. Those are not my best logical hours. But at dusk you can plot itineraries for the next dawn.

Driving to Lake Charles, I resolved to finish my journey full throttle. No giving up. Towns and people would not pass by, nor faces, places, or traces of roadway. There were still goals. I wanted to interview truckers whom I dubbed Knights of the Eighteen Wheelers.

Salinas beckoned. I began negotiating with the National Steinbeck Center in Salinas for permission to sit inside Steinbeck's GMC truck for five minutes. My request was not denied out of hand and went up the chain of command.

Meanwhile, two things happened on the road from Houma to Lake Charles. One almost cost me my life. The other put life back in.

Around eight p.m. one night, a pickup truck whizzed past. In the truck bed were sheets of plywood. The speed of the truck and winds caused the sheets to rise, flutter, and settle. Not good.

The driver stayed in the left lane. Watching those plywood sheets preparing for lift-off, I decided to pass on the right to get away from danger.

Just as I did, one sheet flew out of the truck and landed in my lane on its edge. In that span, the whole trip flashed. All the Montana to Massachusetts miles blazed by. All twenty-six years of my marriage, my wife and three sons snapped past. All hopes, fears, and dreams were suspended.

On I-10, east of Lake Charles, my life hung on the edge of a four-by-eight sheet of plywood. It was the only time I feared for my life the entire trip.

It's amazing how time and motion compress in a second. It seemed certain the plywood sheet, in the vortex of vehicles, would turn on its edge, flip up and through my windshield, ending my life:

John Olson, 57, Poulsbo, Washington, was killed on I-10, 60 miles east of Lake Charles, at 8 p.m. Friday. The fatality came when a sheet of plywood flew from the bed of an unidentified pickup truck that Olson was passing. The plywood crashed through the windshield of Olson's 2008 GMC truck and struck his head and torso.

Olson died instantly, said Louisiana State Police officers. His truck continued several hundred feet into a bayou. Investigators are trying to determine why Olson was in Louisiana on Friday.

Or so my mind believed. Instead, the sheet instantly flattened out, a millisecond before I drove over it. Mother-Mary-Theresa-Joseph-Star-Princess-of-the-Universe, it was close. My heart fluttered for hours. The grim reaper was standing by the roadside that night with clipboard in hand ready to check me off. Somehow, it never happened.

All the New Orleans anxiety, the fingering of pepper spray, the combined futile angst made me laugh, when I realized a sheet of plywood posed the greatest danger in Louisiana.

That is why fiction books and most movies are lost on me. Life itself presents the greatest tales, dangers and snares. They need not be concocted.

****

After that incident, luster returned to the unknowable miles ahead, punctuated that night by the laughter of football referees.

Pulling into a Lake Charles Walmart, I spotted two dozen cars nearby. Normally at the corners of Walmarts late at night, only I parked there. This tight group of late-model cars looked out of place, like a used-car lot.

Around midnight, headlights began bathing my windows. Then laughter filled the night air. Peeking through Gabilan's curtains, I noticed the tell-tale leggings, short pants and striped shirts of high school football referees. Large SUVs were coming from several directions. More referees got out. Jocularity reigned. They were short men, tall men, old men, young men, and of all races.

A security vehicle drove through the lot and I stopped the driver.

"What's going on with the high school referees over there?"

"Oh, they do that every Friday night."

"What? Get together to tell stories?"

"No. Walmart lets them use the lot as a staging area. High schools are spread all over the hell around here and so are the refs. No sense them all driving to games separately and wasting gas. So they come here, jump in one vehicle, go ref the game and come back for their cars."

The refs talked a long time amid reverie. Many were perhaps ex-athletes themselves. Late-season football games are important and these men had done important tasks.

High school sports and I are old friends. Scores of times every year, I'll be in the stands watching football, basketball or soccer. I knew back in my little fishing community on Puget Sound, the games of youth went on that very night. Men in sweaty zebra shirts had refereed.

As much as New Orleans, New York, and Abingdon, Virginia were not home, those high school refs beckoned it. That midnight at Walmart was the best dose of home I could ask for. A few vehicles were still there at two a.m. By morning, they were all gone. How sweet that moment – The Night of the Midnight Referees.

****

Leaving Louisiana for Texas, I debated driving through the night. Steinbeck did on several occasions when his pace had slowed, or a locale seemed inhospitable, or when he didn't want people around.

I wanted to feel deep eyeball dreariness, when the horizon begins to light the dashboard and the Styrofoam cup of cold coffee that sits there. To see a town revive as newspapers hit doorsteps and traffic lights awaken meant driving through the night.

The idea was torpedoed when I tallied the universe of positive thoughts a man could have after midnight driving 2,000 miles from home.

Exactly none.

In timing the Texas portion, I plotted being in a home on Thanksgiving Day because Steinbeck did so among wife Elaine's relatives. I had friends in Fredericksburg, Texas. But way ahead of schedule, deadheading for two weeks in Texas for Thanksgiving, was simply not going to happen.

Still, I would call my friends and stop by. As I neared Fredericksburg, I checked my notes, made a few calls and found my friends now lived in Longview, Texas. I was 250 miles beyond that city. The notion of driving 500 miles to say hello/goodbye to old friends was not going to happen either.

By now I was rock-hard programmed to follow Steinbeck's trail precisely. I would not repeat the Midwest amble of too many faces and miles unrelated to Steinbeck. I headed for the "A" towns: Austin, Abilene and Albuquerque.

****

Most Saturday nights I spent finding a church for the next morning. Arriving late in Bastrop, Texas, I didn't have time. Next morning, I pulled into the first Protestant church I found with a full parking lot.

Worshippers were mostly older folks my wife refers to as "dipped in formaldehyde." The sermon was straightforward, western Gospel. Newcomers were told to pick up a free goodwill gift on the way out.

As I left, none was offered, so I snared it myself off a table – a notebook, pencil and coffee cup. The notebook said "Jesus Is In My Heart" on the front, and "Made in China" on the back.

The straight-shooter pastor had one interesting point: "Are you doing enough, that if you were in a non-Christian country that condemned Christianity, would there be enough about you to prosecute?"

I pondered the question as I headed to New Mexico. The journey had been about Steinbeck, yet had evolved into a spiritual struggle of sorts. What did it all mean?

I prayed, went to church, read a Bible. Then reversed the order and did it again.

Over the horizon lay Brownwood, Texas. Rain pelted as I passed a sign "Mills County Cowboy Church" near Goldthwaite. Several cowboys were practicing bronc riding in a small arena filled with sticky red clay.

A sign said: *No cussing. No tobacco. No alcohol.* If there are 10,000 cowboy corrals in Texas, surely not more than a handful have such rules.

Texas was the first state I didn't sense anyone staring at my truck. Everyone has a truck in Texas with large tires, chrome rims, and belching diesel fumes from multiple tailpipes. If they knew I ran on regular fuel, I'd have probably been escorted to the closest state line: *Don't ya'll come back now, yah hear?*

An auto dealership in Washington state has cars in the front, pickup trucks along the side, or in the second row. In Texas, trucks occupy the front row, the second row, and frequently the side rows.

Leaving Brownwood, I needed propane. A man restocked my supply. He was wearing jeans, pointy cowboy boots, and a blue plaid shirt with button-down pockets. The missing item was a ten-gallon hat.

His name was Alan Henderson. He was sixty, and had a sad air about him, even before revealing his recent widowhood. Somewhere between comparing propane prices and pickup trucks, I asked him about Texas.

"You know Texans. We like to think the sun rises and sets on us. Well guess what? It doesn't. Sometimes we are like New Yorkers. Texans and New Yorkers need to figure out there are other people and places in the world."

That's exactly what Steinbeck proclaimed in *Travels with Charley*. Whether rich, poor, cowboy, millionaire, coast or city dweller, there is only one personal and passionate possession in The Lone Star State. If Texans know anything, Steinbeck wrote, it is that *they are Texans!*

Somehow, Henderson had seen his way through it to claim Texans are no better or bigger than any other American. He had worked construction in New York, Vermont and Colorado. Now he was home.

"My wife died a year ago and that gives your life a

different perspective. But I learned something in each one of those places. I learned that people and places are different. Hell, I still get Christmas cards from people I knew just a short time 30 years ago."

My chat with Alan flowed so naturally, I got in the truck without paying. It didn't take Alan rubbing his fingers together to remind me I had almost pulled a gas-and-dash.

"Heck," I said, "Alan, as long as I'm out of the truck again, I might as well take your picture."

I did and strolled inside to pay. The woman behind the counter had been watching Alan and me shoot the breeze.

"This is going to be a story. It's not often the guy pumping your propane ends up getting his picture taken. Usually it takes five minutes for a fill-up, but once you guys went beyond 10 minutes, I thought you were friends for life."

Some people are like that. Alan Henderson might have been the one person my entire trip, who I felt if I stayed in his town, we might end up good friends. The affinity was instant.

****

Texas might be The Lone Star State – but the star is not alone. It's no accident America's Team down in Dallas has a star logo. In one-half day of tracking, Lone Stars blazed on garage doors, cemetery gates, houses, mailboxes, motels, road signs, license plates, driveway markers, and high schools' facades.

Long stretches of Texas road left my mind to ponder, that when a writer travels, he is not a tourist. You cannot enjoy the forest because the trees are too important.

Is this the town that has an interesting story? You have to look and look intensely. Is every waitress just a waitress? Is every propane seller just a seller?

Looking can be exhausting. During every chance encounter you debate whether to yank out a notepad or tape recorder. If you did that for everyone, you would be on an endless road. Martin Milner and George Maharis on *Route 66*. Every episode taking you somewhere, but never taking you home. Forever a story, never a life.

My Steinbeck journey was work. It was not a busman's holiday. When I returned after eighty days, well-meaning people asked *How was your vacation?* They risked a punch in the nose.

Make no mistake, I relished my journey as pure travel. But it was travel with a distinct purpose that had taken a toll.

I may repeat the Steinbeck journey without a single pencil, computer, or cell phone. People might not hear from me for eighty days. There would be no record of my journey except that etched in memory. That would be a trip. A pure, 180-proof trip and it would be enough.

****

Outrageous things are claimed on the road. Texas towns added to my growing ludicrous list of claims to fame. It's a phenomenon run amok when a city proclaims itself Capital of Something.

Floydada, Texas: *Pumpkin Capital of America.*

Sweetwater, Texas: *The Wind Turbine Capital of America.*

Says who? Where do America's cities go to make such claims? Does a bespectacled man in a nondescript Washington, D.C., office oversee such civic boasting?

How do we know Floydada is pumpkin capital? What if Grand Rapids, Michigan has more pumpkins? Or Sioux City, Iowa bigger pumpkins?

What about Sweetwater and its wind turbine largesse. What if Enid, Oklahoma has bigger wind turbines? Or Visalia, California has more powerful turbines?

Who decides? No one. If you name it, you claim it.

****

When I first hit cotton country, it came out of nowhere. Like a white tornado, cotton descended. Pulling over near Plainview, Texas, I snapped off a cotton stalk that I have to this day.

In northwest Texas, cotton is still king. The excess nestles everywhere. Cotton rests in the arroyos and alleys. It clings to truck axles, car grilles, and fences. On one ATM, I had to pull raw cotton off the touch pad.

Huge ten-ton modules of cotton, ten-feet across, twelve-feet high and thirty-feet long, waited roadside to be scooped up by tractors with giant spatulas on the front and taken to the many cotton co-operatives sprinkled around town.

Plainview residents are surrounded by soft, lazy, ubiquitous cotton. No one in Plainview ever bought a Q-tip swab. They are everywhere.

Between Sweetwater and Amarillo, I saw a reference to Happy, Texas. Pulling over to find it on my atlas, I looked up and saw a wind turbine, oil well, and cotton field.

Texas resourcefulness had taken the full measure of that spot of land. From the air, natural power, the wind turbine. From underground, crude oil. From the surface, cotton.

Road signs warned "Don't Mess with Texas." I did not. Because Texans knew how to wring out every scintilla of worth from a windswept, arid acre of land – air, oil, and soil.

****

On my last day in Texas, I studied the route from Abilene to Albuquerque. I empathized with school kids in the latter town. Imagine Schenectady as well. Those are two cities where you can't spell your hometown until eighth grade.

In leaving Texas, to quote Winston Churchill, it was "Not the end, not even the beginning of the end. It was perhaps the end of the beginning."

My journey had two weeks to go, yet already I knew the journey and its aftermath could not possibly depart from memory. Could John Steinbeck ever see a green GMC truck again without thinking of his 10,000 mile jaunt in Rocinante?

So it was with me. In staking a claim to Steinbeck's

235

journey and reenacting it as best I could, I had invited Steinbeck into the living room of my mind; a spot from which he would never leave.

****

Beginning my journey's homestretch in Winslow, Arizona, I met true royalty of the road; the men and women who move America. Later, they might have been so busy driving *down John's road,* that they drove by without noticing a young man hitchhiking who would not stop until reaching Egypt.

20 THROUGH THE DESERT

It's really for the journey though. The destination
is not that important. Just stick your finger in the air.

Hitchhiker Nathan Lemcke.

****

Even though portions of Texas are arid, only on leaving Amarillo did I actually feel like I was in the desert. At one point, I taped my thoughts. On playback months later, my words proved the desert's grip was complete:

It is flat, desolate earth as far as the horizon. The grass is shoe polish brown. The road is a pure ribbon of concrete.

****

I tended to get two reactions explaining my journey.

You're doing it all alone? How could you go all that way by yourself? Couldn't you find someone to go along?

Those kinds of people cannot spend long stretches of time alone. The idea of 12,000 miles alone was pure craziness to them. Other folks were the polar opposite. I dubbed them Lone Rangers.

Boy, would I love to do what you are doing. Just to get out there, all alone. Man that would be heaven.

By now, I was strung between both views. The lengthening miles strung out time and space. I enjoyed being Kemo Sabe, but even cowboys go to town for supplies. I was ready to come into town.

****

Pulling into Albuquerque November 11, I needed a daily newspaper to find out about Veteran's Day events. In a Walmart parking lot stood Kathleen, age forty-one, from San

Bernardino, California. She was hawking *The Albuquerque Journal.*

On a good morning she sold forty papers and with tips netted twenty-seven dollars. This was a good day. By nine a.m., only twenty papers remained. The comely Kathleen smiled, revealing a distracting toothless mouth.

Kathleen was in town with her husband looking for work.

"What does your husband do?"

"He don't work. There ain't no jobs."

"Why isn't he out here selling papers?"

"If he wanted to, he's got to come out here and talk to these people. I can't do it for him."

"What did you do back in San Bernardino?"

"I used to work in a Holiday Inn."

"Did you try and get similar work here?"

"They all hand out applications, but there are never any phone calls."

"What would be your perfect job?"

"A salesperson over there at Kmart or Walmart, maybe at Target. I've worked at front desks before. I know how to handle money."

I was at a loss. What can you say to a toothless woman, struggling to make meal money selling papers, with a husband who can't or won't work and her dream job is Walmart? I managed a half-hearted "good luck."

****

I went to the main Veteran's Day event near Kirtland Air Force Base in Albuquerque. The ceremony was punctuated by flyovers, some orchestrated, and others just bothersome. After one too many F-16s flew over, drowning out another speaker, the emcee was unapologetic.

"At all our air bases, they say that's the sound of freedom."

There were the usual "speechifiers." A congressman, Albuquerque's mayor-elect, a county commissioner and commander of an air wing at Kirtland.

One speaker referred to the twenty-five million living American veterans.

"Like the rest of you, both veteran and active duty, we signed a blank check to the government of the United States, that could be cashed up to and including our lives."

I'd never heard my own military service expressed so starkly, but what he said was true. The military had once owned a promissory note on my life.

Most speakers referred to the massacre at Fort Hood in Texas just days before where a psychiatrist, an Army major, killed thirteen people – including a dozen soldiers.

The loudest cheers came as a motley crew of twenty young men and woman marched to the dais and enlisted in the military. They earned a standing ovation and became the next batch of promissory notes.

Before the ceremony, I met a wiry, animated retired Air Force colonel named Clay Keen. Clay was eighty-six and was humble about his military career, though I knew it was probably long and laudable. An online bio called Keen a "fixture on the military and civilian aviation scene since joining the New Mexico Air National Guard in July 1947."

Clay served in the Army Air Corp from 1942 to 1946, flying twelve military aircraft on hundreds of combat missions in Korea. He retired in 1974. Then he was a corporate pilot until age seventy and astonished me when he said he was pushing ninety.

"I don't walk like I'm eighty-six, or think like I'm eighty-six, wouldn't you say?"

He was born in New Mexico and never joined the military with the intent of making it a career.

"It was events that did it. It was wars that just kept me moving along."

"What was your favorite plane of all, Colonel?"

"Every damn one of them was good. I would fly anything they would leave the keys in."

Keen gave me a tour of Kirtland AFB, bought me a hamburger for lunch and saw me off. Departing, I asked a loaded question and got a loaded answer. I should have seen it coming. He was a Glenn Beck fan.

"You should listen to him too," Clay said.

"I've turned a deaf ear to talk radio, Colonel Keen. But let me ask, what advice would you give Barack Obama today?"

"Quit. You are a nice guy, but quit."

****

Moving on to Gallup, New Mexico, it proved a major rail nexus. Piggy-back trucks on railcars depicted how deeply China, South Korea and Japan are fused into commercial America. The paint schemes were Yang Ming, China Shipping, Hanjin, Cosco, MOL and Hyundai.

The main drag in Gallup is one of few remaining from Route 66. Lariat Lodge rates were twenty-nine dollars a night; forty dollars if you wanted to pack four people in.

Then Winslow, Arizona beckoned from a line in the 1970 hit *Take It Easy* by the Eagles. I stood on the corner and had my photo taken. On the edge of town rose two, rusty steel columns from the destroyed World Trade Center. A plaque said they were strictly "on loan."

The whole trip I had wanted to chat with long-distance truckers. At Winslow's Flying J Truck Stop, I became a journalist in asphalt ambush. Scores of trucks idled loudly. I approached three trucks and all drivers consented to taped interviews. It was that easy.

Scrubbing his massive truck tires was a young man painted with tattoos. He was Asian and answered many questions with "sir."

I asked him why.

"Because that's what you gotta do in the big house."

"My name is Anthony, I live in Orange County, California."

"How long you been a truck driver?"

"Five years, sir. I own my own truck, sir."

"How many miles you put on in an average year?"

"Let's put it this way – 5,000 a week."

"What are you hauling today?"

"Wood flooring. I'm headed back to California from Tennessee."

"What year is your truck?"

"It is an '03, sir. A Freightliner."

"Did you buy it new?"

"No sir. I can't afford that. I bought it used for $45,000."

"What made you decide to get into trucking five years ago?"

"Well I always loved to drive. It calms your soul."

Anthony, single, is thirty-eight, looks younger and has an apartment that goes mostly unused.

"How much longer are you going to do it?"

"I have a ten-year plan. With this economy, my ten-year plan might take a little longer."

"Where you from originally?"

"I was born in Vietnam. I came to this country when I was ten years old."

"What's the main thing someone needs to know about Anthony?"

"I was a pretty bad kid. I got misdirected in life, but I was a smart kid. I learned ways to make money when I was a young man. Got into trouble. Did some time. I saw what was happening to my friends. Once I served time that was pretty much it. I didn't want to do that again."

"What's the weirdest load you ever had?"

"I once brought a single wood chipper back from Georgia.

That was the only thing I had. A doctor wanted one. It probably cost him $5,000 to ship the thing. It didn't bother me. A load's a load."

Anthony polished furiously.

"I try to look good. It might keep me from getting stopped. Because I am a minority and I have California plates, I might be stopped more often than the next guy."

Did he ever think about giving up the job?

"Yes sir, when diesel went to almost five dollars a gallon. I wasn't making barely anything."

Anthony had two dogs and a satellite radio network to fight boredom.

"On XM radio. I listen to news, music, to a trucker's channel. That one helps you keep ahead of what's going on in the industry."

His used rig had one point seven million miles. He hopes to buy a new tractor that will get considerably more than his current five point six mpg.

Our interview ended abruptly. Anthony said "I have to go, have to make money."

****

Across the lot, a tandem Fed-Ex truck was rumbling. The driver had massive forearms, jowly cheeks and full gravel voice.

"My name is Jim. My hometown is Cuyahoga Falls, Ohio. I've been married for thirty-three years. My wife is in the back. She's a driver too. I have been on the road for forty years. It's all I know. It's bad out here. All you do is sit, drive, eat and get fat."

Jim had the raspiest, cigarette-besotted voice I have ever heard. As if he had smoked since birth. The kind of guy who gets a lung taken out, his larynx removed, who has cancer everywhere and still smokes through a hole in the neck. Jim was that guy.

"How long you been working for Fed-Ex?"

"A month."

"Who'd you work for before?"

"Myself. I was an owner/operator running my own freight. I drove for CNA out of Cleveland."

"In forty years, how many miles you got under your belt?"

"I have no idea."

"It's got to be some phenomenal number. Say two million?"

"More than that."

"Three million?"

"More."

"Four million?"

"Better."

"So, did you start driving right out of high school?"

"No, I didn't graduate. My whole family is truck drivers. I started driving when I was nine, ten years old. My grandfather would put a four-by-four on the clutch pedal so I could reach it. I was born and raised in one of these rigs."

"How's the economy affecting truck drivers?"

"There's work out there if you wanna work. People don't wanna work. It's like driving a Cadillac. You get paid to do nothing."

"You have favorite states you like to drive? Or states you hate?"

"Hate the East Coast."

"For what reason?"

"Tolls."

"How old are you?"

"Almost fifty."

Jim's wife was astounded by that and chirped in the back of the rig.

"Oh wait a minute," Jim said. "I'm almost sixty. I'll have a birthday next week."

"Well that's not too bad, Jim. You only missed by ten years."

"I can't keep track. Each day is another day. And another after that."

"How much longer are you going to do this?"

"I'll probably die in one of these. I had a buddy and he was still driving at seventy-five. All you gotta do is pass your DOT physical."

I asked how often a physical is needed.

"Every year when you're that old."

"But you don't have to take one every year, because you're only fifty-nine?"

"No, I gotta take one every year. I had a heart attack."

"Would you recommend the lifestyle?"

"I dunno. It's a hard life. People don't believe that, but it is a hard life. Thirty years ago, forty years ago, it used to be fun."

"You mean there was less stress before?"

"Well you're younger for the number one thing. You can do more. I used to go a week without sleep. That was many, many years ago. I don't do that no more. We used to have a certain time to go from New York City to Chicago or Saint Louis. You only had so many hours to do that. It was impossible. But you did it."

"You thinking about getting a new rig soon, because this one's a '96?"

"No, I think this is going to be it. This is the one they are going to bury me in."

"Well, I'll let you get back on the road. Can I get a mug shot? Tell your wife to come out and I'll shoot her too. What's her name?"

"Linda."

"How about you Linda, is there ever a time you get scared out on the road?"

"All the time, when he's behind the wheel. He drives too fast."

"You're more law-abiding, huh?"

Linda winked at me as her husband yanked the big wheel and drove away.

****

247

●●▶●●●●●▶●●●●●▶●●●●●▶●●●●●▶●●●●●▶●●●●●▶●●

Something told me to cruise the parking lot a little more. Along the lot's back row, I found a man with a sparkling black rig.

"What's your name sir?"

"Gary."

"How long you been a driver?"

"I started driving in 1975."

"Are you an owner-operator?"

"No, I'm a contractor for John Christner."

"Is it a good company? Looks like they got good equipment."

"This one here's an International ProStar 2010. I just traded in a 2007. I picked this up in April, and already it has 97,000 miles on it. A week ago I was in North Carolina and worked my way back to the West Coast. I was just in L.A. this morning. I'm going to Arkansas."

"What are you hauling today?"

"Chicken bones."

"Not chicken, but chicken bones?"

"That's right. It's going to a dog food company."

"So how much you got?"

"I got 40,000 pounds of chicken bones."

"How many miles you put on in an average year?"

"About 150-160,000."

"So how many days in a year will you be home?

"I like to stay out about four weeks, and then I'll take four days off and I'm gone another month."

"Are you married?"

"Not any more. Been down that road a few times."

"So you've been married more than once."

"Three times."

"What's the worst part about trucking?"

"The winter driving and rush hours in the big cities. No fun, either one. Winter driving might be the worst. That and the way people drive these days. People are insane."

"What do mean insane? Explain that to me."

"People don't know what they are dealing with, with a trucker. They forget I'm loaded up. You've got people in cars that hit their brakes right in front of you. At sixty miles an hour, it takes 200 yards to stop this thing. And that's with all the wheels locked."

Telling the tale, Gary just shook his head.

"What are some of the weird loads you have carried?"

"Well they are not necessarily weird, but there are always the military loads out of Pennsylvania. We never see what's in them, because they don't let us out of the truck. They just put whatever it is in the back of the truck, lock it up, and take it out once we get to California."

"Guess it's a need-to-know basis," I said.

"All we know is, you gotta go. Another one is a load of computers. They've got you routed in advance and a spotter car to follow you. You can't even stop for the first 200 miles. Those are high-priced loads. Cell phones are another high-priced load. Before you leave, they even go over the exact route with you."

"How about my home state? Ever been in Wisconsin?"

"Matter of fact, I was there last year, picking up a load of squash from an Amish farm. They loaded it all up by hand and then I took it down to Gerber Baby Foods in Fort Smith, Arkansas."

"I don't even remember the town in Wisconsin. It was a tiny road, about forty miles out in the country. I thought I was picking this squash up at a loading dock. All they gave me was an address. It was a gravel driveway winding through trees up over a hill. I got up in there and it was a barnyard with no place to turn around. I turned around in a cornfield, or maybe it was a turnip field, I dunno. They had bins and each bin held 1,000 pounds. So I headed out with 42,000 pounds of squash."

Gary said as he left the Wisconsin farm, the Amish headed to the fields with teams of horses.

"It was a little unreal. They told me to have the next truck wait a few days. They had to go out and pick the next load of squash. They were polite and very nice. The women came out and set up a table with coffee and homemade pastries. So, I'm drinking the coffee and eating the pastries, and they're working hard loading the truck and I said 'you guys make me feel bad.'"

Our conversation wound down, but before Gary left in his rig, he said a woman he used to drive with called recently and wanted to form a tandem again.

"I'll have to think about that. Having a woman along and all that entails a lot. I have to think about that. Yes sir."

●●▶●●●●●▶●●●●●▶●●●●●▶●●●●●▶●●●●●▶●●●●●▶●●

****

In Flagstaff, Arizona the next morning, its 7,000-foot elevation meant colder weather. Out of the rack by seven a.m., and on the road an hour later, I drove by Northern Arizona University passing a drenched young hitchhiker in the rain. I invited him aboard.

I have never picked up a hitchhiker in my life. I have never hitchhiked. In fact, I vowed never to do either. The young man had never hitchhiked either. We were both out of our element.

Nathan Lemcke was headed toward Prescott, Arizona.

"What gave you the guts to hitchhike today Nathan? The world wants to know."

"I guess I was trying to prove something as a test that you do when you're young. Also for the experience, because I just read Jack Kerouac's book *On the Road* and it just inspired me to go on this journey. Mainly, I'm going down because it's my little brother's birthday."

"It looks like you were out there for quite a time in the rain."

"I came out at six thirty in the morning. I read on the Internet, getting picked up in the rain is tough because people don't want their car to get wet, but I tried anyway. I was about ready to give up and you came along. A couple people had stopped, but I don't know what it was. Maybe they got scared at the last moment, or weren't going the right way."

I added my own theory.

"They were checking you out. I knew right away you were a student. You had that student look. People, who have been on the road a long time, have scraggly beards and matted hair. That wasn't you."

I asked Nathan would he have ridden with anybody.

"Well, not anybody. I would have told them no. But I was really cold and desperate for a warm ride. But you looked a little like my father and you have a nice-looking car, so I didn't figure you were going to do anything."

"It's a truck, Nathan. Does this rig look like a car to you?"

"Well, it was raining."

I asked Nathan what he was studying.

"Geology, but I'm kind of feeling uninspired by it right now. I don't know if I want a big job when I grow up with big money. I wouldn't mind just getting a little house somewhere. I do like the science of it though."

"So you have any other travel plans?"

"Me and my brother have this plan. We actually got a tattoo together in Arabic. It's maktub. It means 'it is written' or 'destiny' or 'in the stars.' In 2012, we want to travel to Egypt. We are not sure how we are going to do it yet, but that's our goal."

"Why did you and your brother pick Egypt?"

"Mainly, because I read this book *The Alchemist* by Paulo Coelho. A kid in there goes to Egypt and it just seemed like a cool place to go. It's really for the journey though. The destination is not that important. Just stick your finger in the air."

I was surprised when Nathan bear-hugged me at the end of our one-hour ride. I left him roadside in Ash Fork, Arizona thumbing a second ride to Prescott to celebrate his brother's birthday.

See you in Egypt, kid.

****

Down John's road, the question became: Is every town a feature story? I stuck a pin on the map on Needles, California to answer the question and, by accident, poked Houdini's dead wife instead.

21   A PIN ON A MAP

What I set down here is true until someone
else passes that way and rearranges the
world in his own style.

John Steinbeck

****

In December 1960, in southwestern Virginia some 750 miles from New Orleans, John Steinbeck lurched eastbound. Hunched over the gray steering wheel of his GMC truck camper, he gave up on his journey.

In November 2009, while driving 1,750 miles west of New Orleans, I too peered over the wheel of a GMC truck.

Voice to John Olson: *Quit. It's over. The tank is empty. Pull an "Abingdon," the city where Steinbeck abandoned his journey. Do it. Stop thinking, seeing, hearing, or feeling.*

The same voice Steinbeck heard, I heard fully, but rejected completely. Though every emotion demanded it, abandonment was not an option.

****

The time had come to blindly pick a city on a map. My pin-on-the-map concept mirrored reporter David Johnson, of the *Idaho Morning Tribune* in Lewiston. Since 1983, Johnson has written a weekly column, based on opening the phonebook and simply picking a name.

He makes a phone call and convinces the person to be interviewed, in-person, for a feature story. It's a task he has done more than 800 times and written a book called *No Ordinary Lives*.

Steinbeck admitted in *Travels with Charley* that he admired journalists who could arrive on-scene, interview a few key people, and then write a full story. Steinbeck said he admired their technique, he didn't trust it as a mirror of truth. A scene has many truths, Steinbeck argued.

Still, I would pick a town, interview its newspaper editor, and put down what I found true of that town, at that time, in the opinion of one man whose job it is to know.

●●▶●●●●●▶●●●●●▶●●●●●▶●●●●●▶●●●●●▶●●●●●▶●●

My finger landed on Needles, California. Population: 5,290. An old city, hard by the Colorado River. In Needles, I made a loop getting the lay of the land. Parking at the Chamber of Commerce, I walked around on a seventy-five degree, sunny day. Needles seemed empty. I felt like Wyatt Earp with a six-shooter at my hip.

A lady barber advertised eight-dollar haircuts. She sat in front of her shop with bare feet propped up. Under heavy make-up, she looked like Ava Gardner. She'd cut hair in states all over the Southwest and Colorado and at Fort Lewis, Washington while her son served in the Army there.

Logic said start my research at the local newspaper. A sign on the door said it wouldn't reopen for an hour. An older motorcycle sat in the lot. A man circling it smoked feverishly. We chatted about his bike. He asked about my rig.

"What are you doing in town?"

"I'm waiting for the newspaper to open. I want to talk to the editor."

"That's what you been doing, mister. I'm the editor."

He had a few moments and signed off on my idea of finding a story about a city by putting a pin on a map. He was a Midwesterner, from Michigan.

"Your name sir?"

"Robin Richards. Robin like the bird."

"You're editor of what newspaper?"

"*The Needles Desert Star*. It'll be seventeen years in January."

Richards came west in 1982, first working in Douglas,

Arizona, then along the Colorado River since 1989. He became editor of *The Star* in 1993.

"What keeps Needles cooking?"

"We have quite a few railroad workers. Quite a few government workers. This is the last outpost in California as you come east. We have a couple of small industries. Primarily it's a large service sector here."

I asked Richards what had been on his front page lately.

"Health care. Providing health care to California residents this far from the more urban areas is quite a challenge. Concerns exist about Arizona health care providers' level of reimbursement from California insurers or sources."

Though Richards' health care knowledge was vast, I changed gears.

I wanted to know, who from Needles has a claim to fame?

"We've had various and sundry very well-known people who have spent time in the community including Charles M. Schulz, the cartoonist. He included Needles in his comic strip from time to time when he was alive."

"Did he have a summer home or something like that here?"

"Actually, I think he was in grade school while he was here. He remembered the town fondly enough that he included Needles in *Peanuts*."

The receptionist at *The Needles Desert Star*, Tiffiny Limon, said Snoopy's brother in *Peanuts*, Spike, is from Needles. Stretching fame even further, Tiffiny said Harry Houdini's wife died in Needles – sitting on a train.

●●▶●●●●●▶●●●●●▶●●●●●▶●●●●●▶●●●●●▶●●●●●▶●●

That turned out true. Bess Houdini died of a heart attack February 11, 1943 on the L.A.-New York train in Needles. In a delicious piece of irony Houdini would have loved, *The Needles Trick* was one of Houdini's most famous in which he swallowed 150 needles and string, and then pulled them from his mouth neatly threaded. Bess helped with the trick for decades.

Bess had to have died naturally, because Richards told me crime has never been a local problem.

"We get the police reports. You'll find a rock-throwing incident, or a fender bender, an occasional burglary and that's about it."

"Has there been a murder lately?"

"There was a stabbing incident and I believe it was juveniles and proved fatal. There was also a gentleman who escaped from a correctional facility down south. He managed to get as far as Lake Havasu City. He held a couple at gunpoint, took their car, and was trying to evade authorities in Arizona. A passing truck driver got involved and eventually brought the vehicle to a halt on the west side of town. He took off on foot armed with a rifle and fired and hit a police car. He shot one person in the parking lot of a local restaurant. Then he perpetrated a home invasion here in town and the homeowner was armed and stopped him."

"Killed him?"

"It wasn't lethal, but he stopped him. The homeowner was a paramedic and I guess saved the guy's life."

"Let me get this straight. He shot him, then saved him?"

258

"Yup. That was all in the Nineties sometime."

When the crime topic ran dry, I asked about the local economy.

"We probably weren't nearly as hard hit as other areas of the country."

"What is the median home price?"

"The new construction you are going to find in the $150-$200,000 range. You can get a pretty nice home here for about $100,000."

"So what's the big celebration in town?"

Richards said Needles hosts a Renaissance Faire, high school homecoming, Fort Mojave Indian Days, an old-fashioned Christmas in December and a spring rodeo.

"We are very big on parades here."

Each parade goes down Broadway Street, Richards said, which is a Route 66 remnant.

What had kept the editor here for seventeen years? Surely not summer heat above 115 degrees.

"I met my wife along the Colorado River. She's from northeast of Fairbanks, Alaska. We both rather like the weather here. We like the river. If it gets too warm, there are some mountains fairly nearby where we can go cool off."

"What about you, Tiffiny? What's kept you from the big city?"

"My family. I have a sick dad. He's here. I have a boyfriend that has kids. The schools are pretty good here. Probably ninety percent of my family is here."

The editor said schools were excellent with 1,200 students

drawn from 5,000 square miles.

"Needles is arguably the best place in the tri-state area to raise a child. The entire community is very much focused on its children."

He rattled off recent state championships the Needles High School Mustangs had won: boys baseball (2008, 2009); boys basketball (2009), girls basketball (2008, 2009); football (2007); and softball (2007, 2008, 2009).

"We play in the Nevada Interscholastic Activities Association, rather than California leagues, because distances are farther in California to find schools our size."

"Let me get this straight too. You are in California, but are Nevada state champions?"

"Well the Nevada kids are pretty tough. They are not a walk in the park."

I concluded, if it was news, Richards knew it.

Photos were taken and I scampered away after a last question.

"When do you get precipitation around here?"

"Hell, we've got bullfrogs around here that are twenty years old and don't know how to swim yet. That give you the answer?"

****

So went Needles, California on November 13, 2009. It was one newspaper editor to another. But hardly the only Needles a man, woman or child could find that day.

In *Travels With Charley*, Steinbeck talked about how two inquiring minds can visit a place and develop two opinions on what they saw, experienced, or believed is true.

What Steinbeck and I both say is that Needles exists. But a younger journalist in Needles talking with, say, a high school biology teacher, would have an account vastly different from mine.

It's as if a place, set in time and space, exists in many planes at once. Call it Steinbeck's Civic Theory of Relativity. Worked for Steinbeck fifty years ago and works for me today.

****

By evening, I was in Barstow for a rude California greeting. Around eight p.m., I began cruising Walmart looking for a level parking spot. A security guard halted that.

"I hope you're not planning on staying."

"Actually, I was."

"Gov. Schwarzenegger won't let you. State law says no overnight parking by RVs in parking lots."

"You're kidding me."

"Look around, you see any other campers? You can park if you want, but police will be around about midnight or so, and you'll be on your way."

"Well, you got any recommendations?"

"Actually I do. There's a Vons Grocery downtown and occasionally RV owners have spent the night there without being bugged. But don't create a ruckus."

I thanked him, found the grocery mid-town, created no ruckus and wasn't bothered all night.

The next morning I drove Barstow-Bakersfield-Gilroy. West out of Barstow on California Route 58, the road juggled between two and four lanes. It should have stayed four because of relentless truck and RV traffic.

Route 58 meandered straight and true through the Mojave Desert. Sprawling Edwards AFB would pass on the left along with enough cactus and sagebrush to plug a truck's grille.

With my naked eyes, I saw no life in the Mojave – at least not with the eyes of a man seventy days on the road.

After leaving Mojave, California, Route 58 begins a long, slow grind up Tehachapi Pass. From previous trips through, I knew it could be windy. I put two hands on Gabilan's wheel for the gradual descent into Bakersfield.

This would be the last of the barren stretches of Interstate that began in western Texas. No longer would there be featureless roadways, with fast trucks and faster cars passing on the left and the belching diesel snakes of Burlington Northern/Santa Fe or Union Pacific trains on the right.

From then on, I would be surrounded by traffic and sprawl. I-5 would become my main vein – the Interstate from San Diego to the Canadian border would cast a shadow over the rest of my journey.

I would avoid I-5 until I had no choice. The final 1,000 miles of the trip would be a gradual and then sudden return to the geography in which I have lived for the past twenty years.

****

The descent into central California was jarring. Immediately, there were orange orchards and rows of grapes east of Bakersfield, a city of 330,000. It seemed half of them were on the freeway to Fresno. I was tempted to seek once again the two-lane roads I preferred, but Los Banos was my faraway destination. Steinbeck had driven through five decades before.

Bakersfield seemed filled with American Road junk. Huge mounds of old cars waited to be crushed. Six-lane freeways with wire fences caught the flotsam and jetsam. The fences were speckled with fast food and beer packaging, clothes, plastic bags, cardboard, tire remnants and even whole tires.

North of Bakersfield were corporate farms, a particular abomination for a man raised in pastoral Wisconsin, America's Dairyland.

Cows were tightly packed in open yards with not a blade of grass. The cattle stood on huge mounds of manure and dirt. They ate hay and grain delivered mechanically. They entered milking parlors several times a day and then returned to the grassless feedlots – never stepping on pasture. The California Milk Advisory Board ad campaign, promoting milk and dairy usage with billboards of cows standing blissfully in fields of green, definitely stretched the truth.

Forging through Fresno, Los Banos, and finally Gilroy to sneak up on its Walmart for parking, didn't work. Even more warning signs and security patrols. I calculated the distance to Salinas and bolted for Steinbeck's birthplace around midnight.

In Salinas came the same move-out-mister mentality. Helpful shopping-cart jockeys told me about a Salinas truck stop that allowed RVs. They were wrong. The rest stop was surrounded by lighted signs: *Commercial Vehicles Only. Others Park By Permission.*

So I parked street side in a noisy part of town. Men inside a *taqueria* were yelling in Spanish playing cards until two a.m. I did not feel safe in my first night in John Steinbeck's hometown, or welcomed in the whole damn state of California.

It would get worse *down John's road.*

****

How much worse? Jack Kerouac, in his zany coast-to-coast scampers for *On the Road*, could not concoct a more surreal evening than one I endured. It did not come to its merciless end until the man danced with his broom at three a.m. outside Davis, California.

22   SALINAS AND BEYOND

I think 'Travels with Charley' appeals to the dog lovers, the travelers and, maybe, those who are happy to read something of Steinbeck's that isn't so important, philosophical, allegorical, or 'huge' in scope.

Herb Behrens, volunteer archivist at the National Steinbeck Center.

****

●●▶●●●●●●▶●●●●●▶●●●●●▶●●●●●▶●●●●●▶●●●●●▶●●

On a bright Sunday morning in Salinas, California I put on my best clothes. After an hour searching I could not find a suitable Protestant church. Finally, I found one downtown but services had already begun. Arriving late as a regular is one thing, but a tardy visitor appears to be avoiding the collection plate. I drove by.

This would be the day to drive up Fremont Peak. In 1960 John Steinbeck visited it on his last day. I didn't want to risk that if the weather turned sour.

It was an hour drive from Salinas, the last ten miles straight up a narrow and winding road. Water had run over the pavement in recent days, creating gravelly washes. Ascending, my tires slipped on sand and pebbles. For the first and only time on my trip, I activated four-wheel drive.

Trees were draped in mossy aprons and fall leaves nestled in ditches. Roadside sat several horse ranches and a Mormon Church camp. Woodpeckers tapped noisily. Near the summit, grates in the road kept errant livestock from grazing, though they would have found precious little grass near the top.

From on high, I clearly saw why Steinbeck chose it for his Salinas farewell. Speculation exists he never returned to Salinas after leaving in fall 1960.

From the heights, big box stores and fast food restaurants melded together. Nine miles away, Salinas appeared like it must have to Steinbeck five decades before. Checkerboard fields lazed in the distance and up hillsides, wrapping the city in a fertile cocoon.

The horizon loomed endlessly. Using a park map and

intuition, I could see Gilroy, Hollister and the blue Pacific. A yellow bi-plane buzzed the peak and surrounding hills and valleys reminding me of the movie *Out of Africa*. Just before Robert Redford's role dies in a plane crash, he takes Meryl Streep up in a plane and soars over the peaks. Was some modern pilot-lothario taking his lover out on that day soaring over Fremont Peak?

Making a pirouette, I looked east to Maine. Was Brownie the moose making survival preps for winter? To the north, I imagined Montana wondering if Dan and Tiffany still lived in their van, slurping Top Ramen on the lookout for feral cats and dogs to capture for gas money. To the southeast, I wondered if truth-seeking John Carr had reached the end of the Appalachian Trail. Finally, I looked west and saw the end of the West. In the shimmering distance lay Monterey Bay.

Descending Steinbeck's peak proved even more treacherous. Driving up, I was on the inside right lane next to terrain. Driving down, the outside lane yawned like an abyss near drop offs. Guardrails were skinny or nonexistent. I cursed at Steinbeck mightily (the first and only time) for his not describing with more detail how unnerving that drive is for a full-sized pickup truck with 3,000-pound camper aboard.

Back in Salinas, I found the majestic Steinbeck family home at Central Avenue and Stone Street. Painted in hues of blue and green, it has a basement gift shop and serves tea and lunch, but not the day I was there. No tourists were around, so I asked a young man to take my picture. He did so cheerfully, and then panhandled me.

"Got any spare change?"

A dollar, even two quarters would do, he said.

"I'm out," I lied, later feeling chintzy.

Driving to the setting sun surrounded by crop fields, I parked on Foster Road and began walking. Row after row of plants stretched to the horizon, not as far as the eye could see, but nearly.

As the sun set, I let the rich earth sift through my fingers. Not the flaky, sandy topsoil of the Midwest, Salinas' soil is rich and dark, bursting with nutrients. It is also hard, clumpy and if I had thrown a handful at someone, it would have left a welt.

An older Hispanic man driving a small tractor using a machine, punched holes in long black ribbons of plastic over mounded rows. I asked him what was under the plastic, but he spoke no English.

Later I yanked open a section and found budding strawberries. In weeks, I plotted they might be in Chicago, Cleveland or even Sag Harbor.

Evening settled in. I did not want to park again near the noisy truck stop. Earlier, I had driven past the Amtrak station. A young couple in a dilapidated RV climbed out slurping instant coffee. Their rig would not start. I gave them a jump. Barefoot, with bed hair and sand in his eyes, the man told me he was doing a carpentry job in Salinas. They had parked at the Amtrak station for three days without hassle. I vowed to return that evening.

I checked the schedule and knew when a train would arrive. A sucker for railroads, I decided to be there, to smell the diesel and listen to the furtive rattle of the train before it chugged out of town.

When I arrived, a long and graceful Amtrak train had just pulled in. Only a handful of passengers embarked/debarked. The female conductor winked at me.

"Booooard, sir?"

"I wish."

We laughed together. A traveler knows a traveler.

****

The next morning I awoke and pondered why a man in a camper could not sleep at the Salinas Walmart, yet could snore undisturbed in mid-town at an Amtrak station? The answer escaped me then, as it does now.

I drove to Monterey to find the Steinbeck summer home in Pacific Grove. The unpretentious house on Eleventh Street is where he wrote several of his early works. It sat quietly amid fall foliage. Then a quick jaunt through Cannery Row and I found Ed Ricketts' laboratory. I cut two more notches in my tourist belt.

Driving to the National Steinbeck Center in Salinas, I had an appointment with Herb Behrens, the chief volunteer archivist. He made the arrangements for me to sit in Rocinante for five minutes. As I drove up, television crews were taping a politician's press conference who spoke in

English and Spanish.

Herb and his wife Robbie are true Steinbeck aficionados. We chatted about how reliable Herb's plotted Steinbeck route had proved.

Then at five p.m., after the Center closed, I sat in Rocinante – the camper portion. Sadly, the green GMC truck was off limits because too many protective panels surrounded it. I had preferred to sit behind the same steering wheel Steinbeck did. It was not to be.

My curiosity was endless. What were the cab's ergonomics? What view did the mirrors give? Did the radio have knobs or push buttons? How would he have held a cup of coffee? How tight was the fit for Charley?

You can look through the truck's window and see a plaster replica of Charley on the front seat. The cab interior is plain, almost spartan.

There are perhaps ten controls inside the truck: headlights, wipers, gear shift, speedometer, heater, emergency brake and radio are the complete ensemble.

By contrast, inside my 2008 GMC Sierra truck, I once counted ninety-four different switches, knobs, or controls within driver's reach. At night, most controls are back lit and the cab takes on the aura of a Christmas tree inside a Boeing 747 cockpit.

I once encouraged Howard Smith Sr., owner of Wolverine Campers in Gladwin, Michigan, to make a California trek to see his company's most famous product.

"I don't travel that much anymore," he said. "If I ever got

close to California, I suppose I would go see it. You've done a pretty good job of explaining what it looks like to me."

It intrigues me to know I have as a friend a man who, back in 1959, probably had a cameo role in building Steinbeck's camper.

"I got the parts and I put the aluminum on the outside when each one was done," Smith said. "I made one dollar an hour. I was summer help. I got the job because I was a decent bowler. Fred Renas owned Wolverine back then. We were bowling someplace when he said, 'Why don't you come down, I think we might have a job for you.' The rest is history."

Smith does not remember a camper built for a famous author.

"It was probably just a standard one off the floor. He probably bought it from a dealer in New York. Wolverine had outlets on the East Coast back then."

Five decades after Steinbeck and Charley galloped around America, Rocinante still sags. The truck's chassis comes scant inches from the oversized tires.

John Steinbeck paid around $2,000 for his GMC three-quarter-ton pickup truck. The sticker price on my 2008 Sierra (four by four) topped $43,000.

What about the camper price, I once asked Smith.

"I would guess a new Wolverine Camper in 1959 was about $760," he said.

So instead of the $2,000 truck, I sat inside the $760 camper and its paneled interior of an almost orange wood veneer. I sat at Steinbeck's dining table behind an ersatz typewriter, which had not been present during his trip, according to Behrens. I touched the curtains Steinbeck's wife had made by hand.

According to an article in the June 2003 edition of *Vintage Truck* magazine, Rocinante is insured for one million dollars. The figure came from then Steinbeck Center CEO Kim Greer, reportedly also the last person to drive Rocinante.

Steinbeck sold the truck at auction, just after his 1960 trip ended. The entire rig was purchased by Mr. William Plate, who used it for light duty on a spread he owned in Maryland called Maiden Point Farm. Plate donated it to the ever-grateful Salinas museum in February 1990.

Before Rocinante was permanently ensconced inside the building, Greer took it for a final spin, but not without trepidation.

"There was quite a sense of awe about it, to relive that part of history," Greer said. "When I was driving it, I had a huge fear. The only thing I was thinking of was, 'don't mess it up.'"

Archivist Behrens knows where the ignition keys to Rocinante are stored at the museum. Was he ever tempted to start it up?

"The truck has sat so long and the water and oil and gas have been drained, I am not about to try to start it."

Behrens said he receives one or two queries annually about Rocinante, though there was an uptick of information seekers in 2010 – the fiftieth anniversary of Steinbeck's journey.

Few people on earth are as knowledgeable of Steinbeck as Behrens. I asked his perspective on *Travels with Charley*:

I think 'Travels with Charley' appeals to the dog lovers, the travelers and, maybe, those who are happy to read something of Steinbeck's that isn't so important, philosophical, allegorical, or "huge" in scope. I think Steinbeck, when he started to write the tale, some months after the trip, was not as enthusiastic about the book. Just as he was in a rush to get home after he left New Orleans, I think he actually felt tired of the trip before he even got to Seattle. Maybe because he didn't find "The America" he said he was looking for. Or maybe he didn't want to look and couldn't. Maybe the country was just too big for one person to take in, see, observe and comment. Charley makes the whole trip seem worthwhile to the reader.

****

After climbing out of Rocinante and saying goodbye, I sped out of Salinas near sunset. Hell-bent for Napa Valley, my route would be up Highway 101, to San Jose, Palo Alto, San Francisco, across the Golden Gate, around San Pablo Bay to American Canyon – and one final crack at Walmart.

At eight p.m., freeways still pulsed. I maneuvered my rig carefully following a sea of red tail lights. Oddly, the GPS dropped me off freeways and into residential San Francisco. I drove Gabilan like a bulldozer unfazed by narrow lanes, uneven streetcar tracks and Jersey barriers in weird places.

As I neared the Golden Gate, eucalyptus aroma filled my cab. I glided across America's most famous bridge. An hour later I arrived in the city of American Canyon. The Walmart I had chosen looked brand new. I parked in a corner and stopped a security guard trolling the lot.

"Do you think it will be OK to park my rig for the night?"

"Well, I don't know."

"Is this another of those cities that posts No RVs?"

"Well you're not supposed to. But you are pretty small. Pull over in the corner, close to those dumpsters. Make sure you don't stick out in the road. I'll tell the guy coming on at midnight to cut you some slack."

Out walking later, I saw three police officers leaving a coffee shop.

"I hate to bother you, but do you see my black rig and white camper over there in the corner? Am I going to be OK there, or are you guys going to toss me out at three a.m.?"

"Well, it won't be me kicking you out at three a.m. I'll be home asleep. You should be OK. Just blend in man."

Blending didn't work. At one thirty a.m., the parking Gestapo hammered me.

Crash, clunk, thump, whack, crunch at my door.

"Hey bud, gotta move it. California Code says no overnight parking."

"I'm dead asleep. Can you give me fifteen minutes to wake up?"

"I'll give you twenty."

Unbelievable. I was parked alone. No lights, beer, smoking or stereo blaring. Sleeping like a baby, yet I had to go.

Dead to the world, I wobbled out of the rig. The security car was just feet away with emergency flashers on. The guard was no more going to let me sleep in that parking lot than he would allow a Taliban membership drive.

With no coffee, my senses blurry at two a.m., I hit the road. Now I was a true danger to society. With no sense of direction, without a clue, I drove my rig, too groggy to operate my GPS.

Overhead exit signs became hallucinations. The Esparto Exit became Esperanto, a concocted, turn-of-the-century language. The Zamora exit became the Zapruder exit – the man who filmed JFK being assassinated beside the grassy knoll in Dallas.

A few miles later, signs pointed to Sacramento. Why not? I headed there. Maybe I'd make it by morning and see Gov. Schwarzenegger's motorcade. My addled brain said I would lie in front of his limousine and give him a full blast about his stupid "No RV Parking in Walmart" law.

Drifting listlessly toward Sacramento, prying my eyes open, wobbling from lane to lane, I was thankful few vehicles were around.

At two thirty a.m., it hit me. I should not be driving toward Sacramento away from my final talisman – the redwoods. So I exited the Interstate and blithely drove toward the Pacific Ocean.

At three a.m., I could not go one more mile. I found an all-night truck stop and parked. I sat trancelike staring through the windshield. After an hour, too sleepy to sleep, I grabbed my tape recorder to describe the tableau.

What follows is an exact transcription of my mindless ramblings at the Pilot Truck Stop somewhere between Sacramento and hell:

I am dictating this at four eleven a.m., Tuesday, outside a truck stop. California has proven to be inhospitable for the way I'm traveling. I have been traveling for hours. By this time, I am really tired. But I got the munchies. So I go in and get the munchies. The clerk gives me the wrong change. He gives me one dollar too much. So I'm standing there in a stupor and he demands 'I need a dollar back. Give me a dollar back.' At that point, I was so tired, he could have said 'give me the keys to your rig and go sleep in the dumpster out in the parking lot' and I would have done it. I look at the map through fuzzy eyes one more time and I see Highway 113 is coming up. A little shortcut over to I-5. So I get on it. I go by Davis, California and at exactly three a.m. in the morning, Highway 113 becomes I-5, the Mother Road as far as I'm concerned, because I-5, if I wanted to, would take me all the way to Seattle. It goes right through the heart of Seattle. So I drive on thinking how inhospitable the state is, the state that was the native-son state for the man whose trip I am imitating. So I said, Steinbeck drove through the night several times on his trip, I'll drive on too. But my eyes start to burn and I see a sign for a Pilot Truck Stop. A true oasis. It's just after three thirty in the morning. There is this tucked-away spot where you can back in – a couple other small RVs and a long horse trailer are there. So I back in and simply watch the scene in front of me. A young man, highly energized at three thirty in the morning is sweeping the parking lot of cigarette butts, Styrofoam lids, newspaper inserts and whatever bric-a-brac flows through a parking lot at three thirty in the morning. He's just super efficient. He's going at his job with high energy. Every once in a while, he takes his broom and twirls it in the finest manner a drum major with a baton would before a university marching band. He starts pressure washing the parking lot. A multi-colored pickup truck pulls in with four or five different paint jobs. Spinning around the corner, on practically two wheels, the driver gets out, washes his windshield, gets back in, and doesn't buy gas. Drives away. A sports car comes careening off the Interstate, followed closely by a pursuing policeman, who pulls him over in the corner and presumably writes him a ticket. Meanwhile, the kid, the twirling baton guy, checks his cell phone at exactly three thirty-seven a.m. And I'm thinking, who could be calling the guy sweeping and pressure washing the parking lot at the Pilot Truck Stop at three thirty-seven in the morning? His girlfriend saying she loves him? His mother saying bring home a dozen eggs? I'll never know. Meanwhile, the policeman is done writing the ticket for the kid in the fancy sports car and the policeman drives through the lot slowly, right at me, with his lights on, and I'm *thinking, oh great, he's going to throw me out of here too. But he pulls over in front of me, opens up his computer, which police troopers frequently have, finishes up some sort of electronic paperwork or whatever. Meanwhile the guy that he had just ticketed in the sports car, evidently, because he's burning gas at such a high rate, pulls in to the gas station, gets some gas, and then he pulls away to the right, away from the Interstate and disappears. The policeman watches him for a moment and pulls away to the left and gets back on the Interstate. Thirty seconds later, the kid in the sports car, comes ripping by the Pilot Truck Stop, jets up the ramp in the same direction that the police car just went, and I'm thinking, that kid with a fresh tank of gas, and an irritated attitude from having gotten the ticket, might zip down that road thinking that cop is long gone, and that cop might have another Bill of Sale. Meanwhile, I have to go the bathroom. So I go inside the station. It's immaculate. I go to take a leak, and there's like an eighty-year-old man who looks like he just got popped in the face, is, like bleeding from his lower right lip. It's a quarter to four in the morning, he's got paint-speckled jacket, paint-speckled pants, and he's bleeding out of his lip. I'm going, how much more surreal can it get at a Pilot Truck Stop at a quarter to four in the morning? I go to the bathroom, wash my hands, come out to the truck and try to sleep. I was going to go to the Redwood Forest. I may still. I'm so torqued off at California, I might just go up to the Redwood Forest and do what Charley threatened to do in Travels With Charley, pee on one of the redwoods. I might just do that as a human, because I am so torqued off at the Golden State. Good night fans.*

With that, the tape recording ends. Later, re-reading *Travels with Charley*, I found Charley did not threaten to urinate on the redwoods, he did so full force after coaxing by John Steinbeck. Enraged though I was at the whole state of California, I could not pee on a redwood.

****

Where do you expect to find bias or discrimination *down John's road?* Alabama's red dusty roads? Mississippi back country? Among Virginia's good ol' boys? No, it came in Steinbeck's long shadow over California – where talking stupidly to convicts means a quick exit.

23 RACISM AND THE REDWOODS

*To live anywhere in the world today and be
against equality because of race or color is
like living in Alaska and being against snow.*

William Faulkner,
American author.

****

Awakening mid-morning revived and not as angry,
across a field I saw another full RV/trailer park.
The entire trip I wanted to stop and ask a manager:

Was the camp full because of tourists or were people moving in after losing their homes?

Poking around, a sign noted the manager was out. A man near the office offered advice on registering.

"I'm not checking in, but I have questions. I'm from Seattle. I've just driven that rig around the United States for seventy-eight days and noticed a lot of RV parks like this are full. Is it the economy and people getting thrown out of their houses?"

He didn't answer – at first. I asked more questions.

"So you're living here for the winter?"

"No, I hope to get outta here just as soon as I get my eyes checked."

"Where are you from?"

"I was raised out here about fifteen miles, but now I'm out of Oregon. I was headed for Yuma, Arizona, but I had to stop and get my eyes operated on. It's coming along pretty good, don't you think?" he said, removing dark sunglasses.

"Looks good. Did you have macular degeneration, or whatever it is?"

"No, it was some sort of pink shit growing over the eyeball and when they took that off, they found cancer."

"Sorry to hear that."

"I guess I'm lucky I stopped."

"So you talk to many people here? Have they been dumped out of their houses? Do you know their stories?"

Now he began pointing out select RVs and trailers.

"Take this couple here, they drive truck. They got a place up at Clear Lake. And this guy here, he's a fireman. He works up at Cache Creek. Why you wanna know so much?"

"I'm a retired newspaper editor, but I'm still working, doing that journey John Steinbeck took fifty years ago when he wrote *Travels with Charley.*"

"Oh yah."

"Are you familiar with the book?"

"Hell, no. You say he did it in 1960? It don't seem like it's been all that long time ago."

"Interstates were coming in. Pickup campers were coming in. There were only 190 million Americans in 1960. Steinbeck complained about the traffic. Well now, there's like 310 million Americans, he'd really complain about traffic now. How about you? How long you been RVing – that lifestyle?"

"Three years."

"Do you like it?"

"Oh yah, I like it."

I gave him my rant and rave on California and RV parking laws.

"What you wanna do is pull into rest areas. They'll give you up to eight hours before they ticket you."

"But I don't trust 'em. You know what happened to Michael Jordan's father don't you? He got killed at a rest area."

"They killed a guy down here one day too. He'd just gotten out of the Navy, headed home. I think it was at the

Williams Rest Area. Can you believe that? He just had gotten out."

"Did they catch the killer?"

"Shit yah. Dumb son of a bitch had the sailor's ID and all. He went over to Sacramento and tried to get a rental car with the credit card."

I noticed the man had a camper with a black and white map of the United States. Colored in were the states he'd visited in the South and Southwest.

"So are you living in the RV permanently?"

"I am now, yes. It's a 2002. The old lady is trying to get me to sell it and buy something permanent. She's in bad shape anyway. All she can do is cook."

"Cooking's important though."

"Keeps me out of the restaurants."

"What's your favorite state?"

"Arizona."

"Your least favorite?"

"The one we're sitting in right now. Don't like California. Period. It's not run by the right people."

"So Arnold's not your man?"

"That son of a bitch. They should have made a law a long time ago. If you're not born in the States, you should not be allowed to run for office."

"So you knew Arnold was born in Austria?"

"Well, that's just like that goddamn president we got. I voted for that son-of-a bitch, but boy I wish I'd never seen his name on the ballot."

"Why didn't you vote for McCain?"

"That lying son of a bitch. I'd have voted for a dog before I voted for that son of ..."

"What did you think McCain was lying about?"

"Everything, just like the rest of them. So I voted for this goddamned nigger. I figured it'd be a change and he might try to do something. But he didn't do no more than anybody else. I wasted my vote."

There it was. Out in the open. Clear. Concise.

Racism.

The man had tossed the "n" word up and around like pizza dough not caring where it landed. Our conversation evaporated. I didn't want to talk with the guy anymore. He had revealed his ace card and it was worthless.

I had traveled thirty states, 10,000 plus miles and had never heard or seen racism. Not in Chicago, New York, or New Orleans. But in California, as far north of San Francisco as Salinas is south, in Steinbeck's own state, I heard the "n" word. It sickened me.

Steinbeck drove to New Orleans knowing he would find racism in the Cheerleaders. I passed through eighty percent of America and found none. Then it was a gut punch when I heard it at an RV park near Davis, California.

I headed for the redwoods. Why after all the miles did California disappoint so much? It was a riddle.

****

Near Clear Lake, I took a walk in Lucerne, California. Up the road another place was named Nice. I asked a road crew, could it be named after the town in France?

"Yes sir," the foreman said.

As I left Lucerne, the sky turned foreboding and it rained all the way to Arcata. Near Fortuna, a sign read *America's First Certified Organic Brewery*. If you say so.

That night, I stayed in my first hotel in twenty-nine nights. Not since Stonington harbor on Deer Isle had I slept outside Gabilan.

For a month, I had not even been in a house. Nothing but restaurants, truck stops, toll booths, Walmarts, or points of interest. A man needs a house now and then. Needs to at least feel home even if inside someone else's house. My home had been the American Road. For all this country richly gives and suddenly takes, it was no substitute for home.

The penultimate day began in sunny, cool Arcata, California driving to Redwoods National Forest. It did not disappoint. I found a reference to Steinbeck's visit fifty years before. A wooden plaque testified of his respect for the redwoods depicted in *Travels with Charley*. I prefer a different Steinbeck quote than the one listed there:

The vainest, most slap-happy and irreverent of men, in the presence of redwoods, goes under a spell of wonder and respect. Respect – that's the word. One feels the need to bow to unquestioned sovereigns.

Walking The Circle Trail, trees were dripping from rain that had fallen the day before. Red leaves nestled at my feet. A small bridge ran over a creek with a trickle of water. Ferns towering six feet high, framed the trail on the left and right.

There were two Japanese men out walking. Both had lived in the states for awhile – one longer than the other. They wanted to see where you drive a car through a tree. I thought it was on the road from Redding to Weaverville and sent them in that direction. I said it was a Sequoia tree and not a redwood.

I was wrong. There were several redwoods in the area they could have driven through on private land for a fee. Plus others on federal land. Sorry for the wild goose chase, boys.

I walked through a seeming street of trees. One had fallen near the path and was seven feet across at the base. Another smaller redwood grew outward from the side of a hill. At a forty-five degree angle, it reached out forty feet, straightened, and grew, incredibly, straight up another sixty feet.

The Big Tree was at the end of Circle Trail. I paced it at eighty-four feet around at the base. Nearby was another amazing sight. This nestle of trees was probably 150 feet around and was actually three tree trunks intertwined. About twenty feet up, they burst into three separate, but huge trees.

Mesmerized, it seemed primordial, imprinted from before time began. It was a forest of deity and aptly named *The Cathedral of Trees*. It was actually beyond that. A cathedral, for all its soaring, is man-made. This forest, forged by a power beyond nature, stood beyond time and space.

Taking photos, I set down my Styrofoam coffee cup. But after my tree gazing and kibitzing with the Japanese and other folks, I drove away without it. A mile or so gone, I remembered the missing cup. Someone would pick it up, surely a clean-up crew.

My mind would not allow it. How could I desecrate the redwoods with a one-penny Styrofoam cup? I drove back and hiked a quarter mile to retrieve, crumple and stash it.

If I had not remembered the cup until ten miles down the road, I might not have turned back and it would have bothered me. At least enough to look up how long it takes a Styrofoam cup to decay.

As I left the park, near an entrance, sat a gaggle of men in a fire crew wearing orange jumpsuits. They read CDC – California Department of Corrections. Taking a break on the ranger station lawn, many dragged on cigarettes, smoke drifting over their tattooed arms and necks. As was my tendency, I started a conversation.

"No fires to fight today, huh fellas?"

"Nah, but it only takes a spark," one inmate clucked. "Why don't you fire one up and give it a try?"

"You kidding me? They put people away for that."

Instantly, I realized it was not my best choice of words to use with an inmate crew.

I slunk to my rig for the journey home. There was one state between me and journey's end – Oregon. Steinbeck talked about his tires blowing out in Oregon. Given my tires were $400 each and Gabilan was lightly loaded, compared to

Rocinante, I figured Oregon would be event-free.

Near the California-Oregon line, I met a bicyclist peddling north. He had left San Francisco thirteen days before and was headed toward Eugene, Oregon to spend Thanksgiving with his mother. He had eight days to make his turkey rendezvous.

We were both in a hurry after hearing about a coastal storm promising eighty mph winds. Neither he on a bike, nor I with my top-heavy rig wanted to be on open roads with those zephyrs.

Still, I talked him into taking a photo – my favorite of the trip. I sit on a curb, looking toward Pacific Ocean breakers. Highway 101 snakes across a bridge in the background. My big black rig is beside me. Clean and bright with the man-sized emblems "GMC" and "Wolverine."

Miles slammed under my dependable Michelin tires. My log book shows I traveled 398 miles that day, ending at Walmart in Woodburn, Oregon. Anxious to get within hailing distance of home, my GPS showed just less than five hours would have put me in my driveway around daybreak. But that was no time or way to end my journey.

A few miles back, I had filled up with gas at the Oregon-California border. The gas attendant said he and his wife had once lived in an RV for six years.

"We made it through times good and bad," he said. "When you get home, your wife will probably want you to take off for another eighty days."

No chance, my friend. No chance.

****

And so the long trek *down John's road* neared its end. But not before an international cast of men and women slinging *Carne Asada*, gas, pretzels and doughnuts did their thing – proving America is what John Steinbeck said it always was.

24   HOMEWARD IN THE MELTING POT

Who has known a trip to be over and dead before the
traveler returns? The reverse is also true. Many a
a trip continues long after movement in time and space
have ceased.

John Steinbeck

****

This traveler returned home in a gentle rain with classical and country music lilting through the truck. Waking as I had on many days in a Walmart parking lot, I drove to the front of the store in Woodburn, Oregon and had a retired schoolteacher take my photo with my truck flashers blinking.

A quick look at my refrigerator and pantry proved what little interest I had in cooking in the final days. Inside were two boxes of Hamburger Helper, six bottles of water, a few condiments and one mini-pizza; hardly the epicurean delights of a cross-country traveler.

Fuel was low, so I headed across the freeway for a last fill-up. The young Hispanic man who pumped my fuel lamented he had worked for more money across the street, pointing out a shuttered Chevrolet dealership.

****

In many ways you are home once you cross your state line. Roads are familiar. Regional brands of gas and restaurants add comfort. You can turn off your GPS 500 miles from home – *the horse knows the way to carry the sleigh.*

After mingling with the noon crowd in Portland, I drove toward Tacoma, Washington, jockeying for lane position on I-5. Commuters were coming home from a hard day at the office. Me? A hard day at my country.

Halfway between Portland and Seattle, at Milepost 63 near Toledo, Washington, is an oddity called Gospodor Monument Park. Four metal spires rise from a flat plain. They were built for a half million dollars in 2002 by aging Seattle businessman Dominic Gospodor – a real estate and oil pipeline magnate with time and money on his hands.

●●▶●●●●●▶●●●●●▶●●●●●▶●●●●●▶●●●●●▶●●●●●▶●●

One tower is a tribute to Mother Teresa, capped with a wooden statue of Jesus. A second tower is a tribute to Mother Teresa with no Jesus. The third tower honors Holocaust victims and a fourth used to be a tribute to Native Americans and indigenous people. It was topped by Chief Seattle – the Emerald City's namesake.

Recently, the chief came down and a weather vane and U.S. flag went up.

It is just the sort of eclectic roadside artifice that stands for so much you see on American highways. It rises out of the landscape with no explanation. Gospodor had an explanatory sign once, but officials made him take it down after gawkers created unsafe I-5 back-ups.

Gospodor wanted to expand the site with tributes to Jonas Salk and drunk-driving victims. No law could stop him, just as it couldn't stop the burial of psychedelic Cadillacs, hoods down in dirt outside Amarillo, Texas.

Sadly, Gospodor died in 2010. The mayor of the town nearest the odd towers, said someone ought to put a hamburger stand beneath them.

****

As my trip wound down, I created a microcosm of America in my final thirty-six hours on the road. In short time, I had:

- Eaten in a Mexican restaurant in Arcata, California.
  The waiter spoke "business" English.

- Chatted with two Japanese men in the redwoods. Both had lived in the U.S. for extended times.
- Had my final gas pumped in Oregon by a Hispanic man.
- Stopped in Tacoma for Bavarian treats at a cafe and bakery operated for decades by German expatriates.
- Eaten donuts in a shop near the Tacoma Narrows Bridge in a store run by Vietnamese siblings.

Embedded in those final miles lurked an undeniable fact. The United States is what it has always been – the greatest ethnic melting pot the world has ever known. John Steinbeck believed that too.

I did business with Hispanics, Japanese, Germans and Vietnamese as naturally as a seventh-inning stretch at a July Fourth baseball game.

****

Finally, in a thin rain, at three thirty p.m. on November 19, 2009 with 12,673 miles logged on the odometer, I maneuvered the big rig into my driveway – eighty days after leaving. I had burned exactly one quart of oil.

For all my fears, I never once used my pepper spray. Not even close. For all my intense focus on John Steinbeck, Rocinante, and *Travels with Charley*, only one person asked me what Gabilan meant written on my camper's side. To Becky Smith, wife of its chief builder – *thanks for asking.*

There are opposing photos of my exact moment of homecoming. I held a small digital camera over my steering wheel and took images of family and friends awaiting me. At the same moment, from my porch, they took photos of me.

Each photo captures the photographer in the other. Had I gone off to capture the country and instead been captured by it? Had I thought I was looking for the consummate American, when all along, I was the one being found?

There had been eighty journeys within the whole. Each was its own daily, emotional capsule. There were 12,673 one-mile treks. Each segment had rhythm, rhyme, beauty, ugliness, purpose and banality all its own.

The overarching quote, anyone with a hen's scratch of knowledge of *Travels with Charley* knows, is John Steinbeck's seminal line:

We find after years of struggle, that we do not take a trip; a trip takes us.

Did I take an eighty-day journey, or did eighty days take me? Did I plan anything, or was it all pre-ordained by some unseen Rand McNally programmer?

As the pastor in Hillsdale, Michigan said in late October, are there really people in hell urging you to take or not take a certain course? Was it Steinbeck himself who led me to Brownie in the far-flung Maine woods? Did Charley's spirit listen as I interviewed ex-con Dan and ex-mental patient Tiffany in Billings, Montana? Who was it that steered Dave, schizophrenic, unforgettable Dave, to push his shopping cart past my truck in Groton, Connecticut?

In the end, I both controlled the trip and was controlled by it. It was two universes in one. I am better for it.

****

The one question long-distance travelers, including John Steinbeck, are often asked upon return is inevitable. What are Americans like today?

I truly don't know and neither did John Steinbeck. I met a finite number of people and they told me true lies, or lies that were true. But do the people I met represent all Americans?

Hardly. I never drove through Kansas, Missouri, Nebraska, Iowa, the Carolinas or another dozen states. I saw an American subset. A subset now reduced by several people I met who have since died.

Every mile traveled was altered the moment I churned through it. Every second spent on the road is gone for all time, yet captured forever in my mind. As time passes, the memories will blend together, get tossed upon each other until not even I, in dolting old age will recall the trip correctly.

As for John Steinbeck, in 1960 he took guns and fishing poles to blend in. I drove a GMC truck with a Wolverine Camper, which did not blend in well at all.

He regaled his Maine guests in Rocinante with whiskey and Cognac. My homeless guests inside Gabilan in Montana were treated to Egg McMuffins and orange juice.

For comfort, he stayed at the swanky Ambassador East Hotel in Chicago with his perky wife Elaine. After twenty-nine straight days on the road, I luxuriated, alone, in a Motel 6 in Arcata, California.

Still, we had one thing in common as we drove *down John's road*. On his trip, John Steinbeck claimed he was never recognized – not once.

Imagine that.

Neither was I.

EPILOGUE

When you have completed 95 percent of your journey,
you are only halfway there.

Japanese proverb.

****

T he math above is slightly skewed, because a journey never ends. It has a half-life that gets smaller, but never disappears.

When John Steinbeck returned from traveling with his beloved Charley, an invitation was waiting to John F. Kennedy's Presidential Inauguration. On January 20, 1961,

Steinbeck sat on the Capitol steps in frigid Washington, D.C., rubbing his wife Elaine's cold feet as JFK said:

And so, my fellow Americans: ask not what your country can do for you – ask what you can do for your country.

When I returned, no White House invitation was waiting. Barack Obama had long been inaugurated. Instead, I spent the time emptying Gabilan of clothes, weekly files, bedding, tape-recorded interviews and 1,000 digital photos.

Within weeks, I sold Gabilan to my brother who has two young boys. The big black GMC truck and Wolverine Camper will give them years of pleasure.

John Steinbeck sold Rocinante as well. It was auctioned off and used on a Maryland farm before its donation to the National Steinbeck Center in 1990.

Steinbeck lived another eight years, dying December 20, 1968 of heart failure. Charley's many maladies on the 1960 trip presaged his death in 1963. Steinbeck is buried in Salinas; Charley reportedly on Bluff Point in Sag Harbor, Long Island.

****

Eighteen months after my trip, this is what I know of the people I met.

John Carr abandoned his Appalachian Trail walk two weeks after I met him, sounding like a weary Forrest Gump.

"Basically, I got tired of walking," Carr e-mailed me in 2010. "I had always told myself, if I got bored of it, or if I was just doing it for the sake of doing it, I would quit. That's exactly what happened."

Later, John joined the Marine Corps Reserve.

Retired coal executive Gene Matthis of Abingdon, Virginia, died five short months after telling me *Travels with Charley* was his favorite Steinbeck book.

In November 2010, hitchhiker Nathan Lemcke reported he and his brother are still saving money for a November 2012 trip to Egypt. I wonder if upheaval in Egypt has tempered those plans.

I sent a 2010 Christmas card to the Schwartz family in Indiana. The Amish family did not send one back. Maybe that's another *English* tradition Amish don't participate in.

Finally, Brownie the moose faced good odds in the 2010 hunting season. Maine wildlife officials reported 2,475 hunters tagged a moose kill out of an estimated herd of 29,000.

Hang in there Brownie.

****

I have come to believe my Steinbeck trip mimics life itself.

At the risk of sounding hopelessly philosophic, life meanders like a ship at sea. The wakes and the ripples we create simply disappear. The important thing is that *you* remember being there.

When I am asked for the seminal moment of my trip, this is my answer. It came just after midday, Monday, October 19, 2009, while I churned through Calais, Maine on U.S. Route 1.

On the right, a small Laundromat flashed by. In front, stood two middle-aged women, smoking cigarettes and having an animated conversation. In the background, among the trees, an old house nestled against a hill.

Try as I might, the image will not fade from memory. It is stuck on a veritable lazy Susan in my mind. A dingy Laundromat, two agitated women, two cigarettes, a truck camper glides by, the clothes tumble inside washers and dryers. The cigarettes are stomped underfoot, the big black truck disappears down the road, and two arguing women dip inside the dank Laundromat.

The moment ends.

But does it? The scene means nothing, yet everything. That moment in Calais, Maine, is connected to every moment before and after in a cosmic timeline. The road through Calais, Maine is connected to the road in front of your home, my home, every home.

All seconds, of all time, are connected to the one in Calais, Maine. Who connects them? Me? The two women in Calais? You, the reader?

During my 2009 trip I wrestled with God and faith, later struggling with how much of that tension to place in the book. I didn't want to offend anyone of another faith, or someone with no faith. To leave it out would have been a lie.

●●►●●●●●►●●●●●►●●●●●►●●●●●►●●●●●►●●●●●►●●●●●►●●

I wanted to know then, and also now; what do individual seconds mean? What about that moment in Maine?

Did John Steinbeck ponder the seconds and moments of his 1960 journey? Steinbeck was not an overtly religious man, though many of his books are filled with Christian imagery: *Grapes of Wrath, East of Eden,* and *To a God Unknown*, are certainly not the least.

It's inconceivable John Steinbeck would not have pondered deeply all the connected seconds. In Chapter Thirty Four of *East of Eden,* Steinbeck writes of life's most important story. He concluded: mankind is forever stuck in a net of good and evil – and that is the "only story" any man, woman, or child ever has a chance to write. Hard to disagree with Steinbeck on that.

To me, the one who determines good or evil is a power beyond our knowing. When a journey – our journey – is over, it has only begun. All that happened, every person you met, ever mile you drove, all the good or evil, matters to God.

That second in Calais, Maine on October 19, 2009 counts. It matters to Him now and forever, exactly what happened, every second – *Down John's Road.*

APPENDIX ONE

Ruby with the White Dress On

But now I heard the words, bestial and filthy, and
degenerate. In a long and unprotected life I have
seen and heard the vomitings of demoniac humans
before. Why then did these screams fill me with a
shocked and sickened sorrow?

John Steinbeck, on hearing the
"Cheerleaders" in New Orleans.

****

In the fiftieth year after John Steinbeck witnessed the racist "Cheerleaders" in New Orleans, Steinbeck could not come to Ruby Bridges. Instead, Ruby Bridges came to him.

On August 8, 2010, at the National Steinbeck Center in Salinas, California, Bridges – now Ruby Bridges Hall – was keynote speaker at the Thirtieth Steinbeck Festival. About 300 people listened raptly as she recalled events at William Frantz Public School in New Orleans in fall 1960. Her talk was titled: *My Journey Up the Steps.*

I flew to Salinas in August 2010 and was sitting on the outside of row three in the room where Ruby spoke.

Now middle-aged, Ruby described her first day of first grade in 1960, the only black student integrating an all-white school. It was not Ruby's first day of school. The year before, Ruby had attended an all-black kindergarten.

"I always say to kids, it was a whole lot different than your first day. They think that somehow my parents could have prepared me for what I was about to walk into. But you can't. There is just absolutely no way to prepare a small child for what I saw that day. So my parents didn't try. They only said: 'Ruby, you are going to a new school today and you better behave.'"

Bridges said her first memory was "four very tall white men came to the door." They were U.S. Marshals anticipating protest at the school in the Lower Ninth Ward. She said school officials had gone door-to-door looking for black parents to volunteer children to integrate. Tests were given. Ruby tested high and was chosen for William Frantz Public School.

"But that test was set up to eliminate kids," Bridges said. "Only six kids passed the test. I take pride in saying they were all girls. Boys just hate that."

Bridges said only two schools were chosen for integration.

"Those two schools were located in the most racist parts of town. It was set up to fail."

Three students were to attend each school. When day one arrived, parents of the other two students chosen for William Frantz Public School changed their minds.

"It was too late to find more volunteers. That is how I ended up going to school alone."

The day arrived, the men with yellow armbands knocked.

"We are U.S. Marshals. We have been sent by the President to take you to school."

Bridges got in the car in her starched white dress and was driven to school past people lining streets behind barricades. Police were everywhere. Of particular interest to the press were the young and middle-aged white women who spewed the worst invectives at Ruby Bridges.

They came to be known as The Cheerleaders. John Steinbeck wrote at length about them in the final chapters of *Travels with Charley*. He was physically sickened by the women's behavior.

Ruby Bridges told the Salinas audience, that in November 1960, when Steinbeck watched her enter the school, she was too young to understand her place in history.

"I actually thought it was Mardi Gras. I remember thinking we are in a parade. The minute they opened the door, and grabbed me and walked me toward the front stairs, I remember looking at the building and thinking, oh my gosh, it's huge. Then I thought, I am so smart, I am going to college."

Bridges was six years old.

"I was not afraid at all. I remember hearing things. The screaming and shouting. I did not even think they were shouting at me."

The crowd that had been outside soon rushed inside. On that day, 500 white students were disenrolled by angry parents.

"They were pointing at me. Shouting. Their faces were really angry. They looked really upset. There were kids with them."

"I sat in the principal's office most of the first day. I said, 'this must be how college is.' Finally someone came in and said school is dismissed. You can leave. I remember looking at the clock and walking down the stairs. I remember thinking, college is easy. Nothing happened that day. Nothing at all. We got into the car and drove home."

The second day was more of the same, Bridges said.

"They drove us to school. But the minute we turned the corner on the second day, the crowds outside the school had almost doubled. I remember they were screaming a chant. *'Two-four-six-eight-we-don't-want-to-integrate.'* I remember that because it rhymed. When I got home, my sister and I jumped rope to it. I didn't even know what integrate meant."

"When I got inside on the second day, it was so quiet. When we were walking up the stairs, we could hear all of our footsteps. At the top of the stairs, I remember it was so clean. I could see myself in the floors. That was totally different from the all-black school."

The U.S. Marshals walked Bridges down a long hall to a classroom. The door opened and a teacher walked out. She introduced herself as Mrs. Henry, her teacher.

"I remember looking at her and my first thought was she's white. I had never seen a white teacher before. She looked like everybody else outside that was screaming. I didn't know what to think of her. But she said 'come in and take a seat.'"

Ruby said the classroom was rows of empty desks. She thought her mom had sent her to school early. Bridges thought surely other students would eventually arrive.

"So she began to teach me. She did everything. She played games with me. She read stories. We worked on drawings and making all kinds of things. She really made school fun. I loved school."

"I have to say, that the lessons I learned every day in that classroom, weren't my studies. They were fun and I enjoyed them. But the lesson I learned was the same one that Dr. King was trying to teach all of us. We should never look at a person and judge them by the color of their skin."

Ruby said Mrs. Henry "showed me her heart. She loved me. And I loved being with her. That love shaped me into where I am today. I am not prejudiced. I know that for a fact. To this day, I still feel that love. I remember looking at her and understanding that she was different. She is still alive. She lives in Boston. She is still my best friend. We built a relationship that lasted a lifetime. She is like my mom."

Bridges' education commenced, albeit alone.

"I couldn't go to the cafeteria. I could smell food cooking every day. But they wouldn't let me eat that food. Because someone in the crowd was always threatening to harm me or someone. 'We are going to hang her. We are going to poison her.'"

The U.S. Marshals told Bridges' parents to prepare her food.

"So I never was allowed to eat at the cafeteria. But I smelled food. I thought the kids were at the cafeteria. If I could just get to the cafeteria, I could see the other kids."

Eventually, Ruby was shown the cafeteria. It was empty.

"Finally I figured it out. They were boycotting the school. What was happening was that there were some white parents who tried to send their kids to school. There is some video footage of them being interviewed by reporters. What they said was that, at night, their neighbors threw bricks and rocks through their windows. Their husbands had been fired from their jobs. They were never protected by the U.S. Marshals, like I was. They said they were being harassed. They said people were burning crosses on their lawns. So eventually they would take their kids out of school."

Though brave white parents were still bringing their kids to the school, Ruby never saw them.

"The principal, who was part of the opposition, she would take the kids and she would hide them."

Ruby's teacher, Mrs. Henry, eventually confronted the principal.

●●▶●●●●●▶●●●●●▶●●●●●▶●●●●●▶●●●●●▶●●●●●▶●●●●●▶●●

"The law has changed. You are hiding those kids from Ruby. If you don't let those kids be with Ruby, I am going to report you to the superintendent."

Meanwhile, there were repercussions for Ruby's family.

"My father lost his job. There were longshoremen that lived on our street. They got together and they actually brought money to my father every weekend, because they would all get paid on Fridays. They would bring food. It was truly a community, something that we don't see in our communities today."

Ruby said there was plenty of community back in 1960. At least, in the black community.

"Every day I rode to school with the U.S. Marshals. Because it was actually a short walk, everybody, in almost every house on that street, would come out every morning and would walk behind the car. So even though I was driven to school, there were neighbors that walked me to school by walking behind the car."

During a short question and answer session in Salinas, Bridges was asked about Steinbeck's observations in *Travels with Charley*. Did she actually skip up the steps and into school?

"I'm a lot slower today. But he was probably right because, I loved to skip and hop. I tried to explain to you what that day was like. I saw things in a totally different light. I guess it was just the innocence of a child. Being naïve. So maybe that protected me."

It would take time for white parents to let their children attend William Frantz Public School. Over time, they returned and Bridges would spend six years at the school.

There were no kids in her class the entire first grade. She spent the whole year alone. For second grade she had a different teacher. Mrs. Henry had left.

"She was gone. She was not protected. The other teachers in the school really didn't want to have anything to do with her. In a sense she was ostracized."

Ruby was having a hard time figuring out the empty school, the tall white marshals, the women swearing at her, the scrutiny her family was undergoing. She couldn't arrange it in her mind until another young white boy, made it all make sense.

"He told me, I can't play with you. My Mom said I couldn't. You are a nigger. I thought what if my Mom would have taught me that way? What if my Mom had said don't play with them? He's Asian. He's Hispanic. He's Jewish. He's Indian. He's white. He's mixed-race."

It was then little Ruby Bridges, with the white dress on, figured it all out.

"This isn't Mardi Gras. He made it all make sense. I didn't have to figure it out anymore. We never became friends."

Ruby Bridges eventually went to college and spent a career in the travel industry. It would be nice to say she was rarely touched by racism or violence again. She married, stayed in New Orleans and had children.

"I told you that I have four sons," Ruby told the hushed Salinas audience. But now she has only three.

"I lost my oldest son. He was murdered. He was my friend. It is a pain that I cannot ever begin to describe to you. Because it was evil."

Ruby described how in April 2005 her second son was in an incident.

"He was on the Interstate. He ran off the road. Nobody stopped. All they saw was a bleeding man dripping in blood. He was hit. It was twenty-five minutes before anyone stopped."

After the accident, Ruby said her oldest son could not let it go even though his brother had survived. He began to investigate why no one stopped. Why no one helped. He was told to let it go, but could not. It cost him his life. He was shot eleven times.

Ruby Bridges said her son's murder was not because he was black.

"It had nothing to do with racism. It was evil. And it comes in all shapes and sizes. Evil doesn't care who it uses."

Ruby travels regularly telling her life story.

"I see the kids. Sometimes I am in two schools a day, all across the country. They love the story of Ruby Bridges. It's about loneliness. It's not about me. It's about the story. It's about the message."

That message Ruby relayed to the Salinas audience in August 2010, including me.

"It is happening all around."

"We keep racism alive."

"We keep spreading evil."

"We keep passing it on."

"We keep destroying."

Bridges was asked how she could possibly stay positive after losing a child to violence.

"If I stayed in that place, I wouldn't be here today. It was a dark and depressed place. I got through it with prayer and the help of my other sons. I do know that each and every one of our kids comes into the world with a clean, fresh start in life. A clean heart."

"The problem is evil. It's killing us all. I believe that racism is a lot more dangerous today than it was back then. Because today, you can't see it. Back then, you could see it. I saw it in front of that school."

"Racism is just evil. It comes in all shapes and colors. It looks like you and me. Evil is not prejudicial. It doesn't care who it mistreats. It doesn't care."

Ruby Bridges Hall finished her speech in Salinas to a standing ovation. She is a pretty, immaculate woman. Quiet, almost regal in bearing, she walked passed me, I held out my hand to shake hers. She accepted.

"Ms. Bridges, I was at your old school last year. It seemed all under construction."

"That's one of my projects. It's part of my foundation. Part of the work I do."

Then she walked on, into a world vastly different than John Steinbeck's, but also vastly the same.

APPENDIX TWO

In summer 2009, during two phone conversations with Thomas Steinbeck, he gave advice for traveling properly, especially if recreating his father's 1960 trip:

1. Buy tie-downs – use them in a storm.
2. Always set the emergency brake. My father didn't, and his truck actually moved once in a windy storm.
3. Call someone every day.
4. Keep a daily log, like a ship at sea. Make note of the weather, winds, rains, road conditions, and temperature. It will help you remember the trip and looking at the log will help you drag things from memory.
5. Go minimal. Buy everything else at Target.
6. Think about handling fatigue. Get in shape. Exercise. Weariness and loneliness will set in. Be prepared for it.
7. Know why you are going. There are people out there right now, by the thousands, taking my father's very same journey and they don't even know it. And they also don't know why.
8. Take a laptop. Take a good cell phone – not a cheap one. Get one that works everywhere.
9. The trick is to be safe. An RV or camper is an everyday occurrence out on the road. Once you are inside the city, then you stick out.
10. Get to a hotel/motel early and stay late. Take advantage. Use every damn towel they have.

●●▶●●●●●●▶●●●●●●▶●●●●●▶●●●●●▶●●●●●▶●●●●●▶●●●●●▶●●●●▶●●

ACKNOWLEDGMENTS

W hen a writer finishes a book, he finds a committee of support has formed. *Down John's Road* is no exception.

On September 9, 2010, I learned my father had died at age 84. Of all the desires, morals, values and belief systems he put into me, the love of travel is deep.

Thanks for all of it Dad.

I am grateful for the help, on many occasions, of Herb and Robbie Behrens, volunteers at the National Steinbeck Center in Salinas, California.

Thomas Steinbeck provided valuable insight into his father's 1960 journey, during two phone interviews in 2009 from his home in Santa Barbara, California.

I thank Terry Finnerty for his camera skills and his wife Sandy, for providing the GMC ball cap that rode every single mile. I have never met an Ohioan I didn't like.

I thank the crew at the Silverdale, Washington Census Bureau, who provided a lifeline in the time between finishing my 2009 trip and beginning the writing. They restored my road-weary soul, especially Jonathan, George and Marilyn.

I am indebted to Howard Smith Sr. and his entire extended family at Wolverine Campers, in Gladwin, Michigan. My friendship with the Smiths goes far beyond our business relationship.

No man listened more to my dream, for nearly three years, than neighbor and good friend Larry Smaaladen. That fifty dollars bought a very good steak. May we caucus forever.

During final stages valuable insight and assistance was provided by Dave Bolthouse, Judy and Tom Driscoll and Michelle Olson. Mark Dallas kept me on track at the outset.

Editing help and advice came from best-friend-for-life Chuck Peterson. His friendship of fifty years, has been a beacon.

I thank my brother Paul Olson for his final chop and fact-checking. You made every page better and more accurate.

I thank my sons Phillip, Nicolas, and Evan for encouragement and technical know-how. Your computer savvy knows no end.

To Zorro, my dog, who lost his shot at notoriety: *Z-dog. A man needs a best friend in tough times. You were mine.*

Finally to my wife Lisa, already mentioned in my dedication. I say again: *I simply could not have done it without you. Your courage knows no limit.*

Poulsbo, Washington
April 2011

About the Author

John Olson is a retired journalist living on Puget Sound, west of Seattle. After eight years in the U.S. Navy, he graduated from the University of Wisconsin – Madison with a journalism degree in 1987. He was a radio news editor for the Voice of America in Munich, Germany. In 1992, on Bainbridge Island, Washington, he co-founded *Mission Network News*, a religious news program still heard on 1,000 stations worldwide. For 14 years, he was a newspaper editor in Kitsap County, Washington, retiring in 2003. *Down John's Road* is his first book.